A Backyard Book of Spiders in Maine

DANA WILDE

A Backyard Book of Spiders in Maine

Book design by Chelsea Ellis

ISBN 978-1-943424-52-8

LCCN 2019950486

North Country Press

Unity, Maine

This book is for Bonnie, Jack, and Silas,
not all spiderlovers, but definitely loved.

Contents

Special Topics

from September

... Perhaps a glance
might spy a black and yellow argiope,
bright as a star winks in black eternity.
Banded legs spread as if to pounce,
she crouches in her zig-zagged canopy
like a tiny terrible tiger whose stripes
and spots blaze with more pure fun
than we realized in all our whiny gripes
God might favor upon such a little one.
With every roaring swoosh
the bramble where our spider's napping
at dead center of her deadly mesh
whips in a fevered spasm so fierce
to us we'd pray and plead and curse,
but to her seems but a gentle lapping
over hills and valleys of forever
in the never we call the universe.

by William Hathaway

Preface

This is a general interest book by a general interest backyard naturalist for general interest readers and naturalists. The information here is drawn from a wide range of sources: from popular guidebooks, to arachnologists' guidebooks, to scholarly papers, to personal communications with professional spider and biological sciences people. The author is not a scientist.

The principal sources of factual information are: Richard A. Bradley, *Common Spiders of North America* (2013); Rainer F. Foelix, *Biology of Spiders* (2011); W. Mike Howell and Ronald L. Jenkins, *Spiders of the Eastern United States: A Photographic Guide* (2004); Daniel T. Jennings and Frank Graham, Jr., *Spiders (Arachnida: Araneae) of Milbridge, Washington County, Maine* (2007); and D. Ubick et al., eds., *Spiders of North America: An Identification Manual* (2017). An alphabetical list of works consulted is included at the end of the book.

Also frequently consulted was an early version of "A preliminary checklist of Maine spiders (Arachnida: Araneae), including species found elsewhere in New England and in Atlantic Canada," primarily the research work of Daniel Jennings with help and support from former Maine state entomologist Charlene Donahue and staff of the Maine Forest Service. This checklist was in the last stages of its preparation at the time this book went to press in 2020 and was expected to be published later in the year, so information referred to here was taken from an incomplete version, and tallies given for some spider species may differ from the published list.

Details on the etymologies of spider genus names are taken mainly from H.D. Cameron's "An etymological dictionary of North American spider genus names," Chapter 75 of *Spiders of North America*. Guidance on common names came from the American Arachnological Society's *Common Names of Arachnids* (2003), along with dictionary consultations.

The author had generous personal communications with Dr. Richard Bradley, Dr. Kefyn Catley, Dr. Jerome Rovner, and University of Maine Cooperative Extension entomologist Don Barry, who all offered help to one extent or another with factual details and identifying spiders in photos. Daniel Jennings generously read and made suggestions on a magazine article that was the forerunner of this book in 2013.

The author took most of the photographs; for those photos he did not take, the photographers are named in the captions. Most of the photos were taken in Unity and Troy, which are adjacent towns in northern Waldo County, Maine; other city and town locations are indicated in the captions.

The animals in the photos are identified to a reasonable degree of confidence to family, genus, and/or species. Only two of the spiders pictured in these photographs were keyed out under a microscope and positively identified, and those are the dictynid shown resting in its vial during Dr. Catley's summer 2017 spiders seminar at the Eagle Hill Institute in Steuben, Maine, and the short-bodied cellar spider (*Spermophora senoculata*), which I found in my basement and enlisted Dr. Richard Bradley's help to identify it. All the others were photographed in the wild or in a container and then released. So the identification of the dictynid and *Spermophora* are certain, and the rest confidently resemble the identification to the eyes of experienced and expert arachnophiles, including the experts at the SpiderID and BugGuide websites. Any errors are the author's responsibility alone.

And just to be clear: The author of this book holds advanced degrees in the humanities, but no degrees in the sciences. He has collected information from scientists and framed it from the perspective of a person who loves the ecologies, connections, fascinating details, and metaphors inherent in the natural world, and in particular, the incredible world of spiders.

Acknowledgments

Many thanks to Dr. Kefyn Catley, Dr. Robert Nelson, and Maine Master Naturalist Donne Sinderson, for reading the manuscript of this book, making corrections, and offering very helpful suggestions, and to Joanna Young, who designed the front cover, and Ellen Hathaway for design suggestions. Special thanks to James Reben for allowing the use of some of his painstaking photos of spiders, and to William Hathaway and Leslie Moore for allowing the use of their poems to frame the book's core, inner interests. And also, a grateful nod to my colleagues in Dr. Catley's spiders seminar in July 2017, whose enthusiasm and knowledge charged my notes from that week. Some of the special topics pieces in this book were first published in different form in the Backyard Naturalist column of the Central Maine Newspapers.

Introduction

1. SPIDER BASICS

First, spiders are not insects. Spiders have eight legs, while insects have six. Spiders have two body sections: the abdomen (the rear end, also known to arachnologists as the opisthosoma) and the cephalothorax (or head, also known as the prosoma). Insects have three body sections: head, thorax, and abdomen. The spider's cephalothorax is one unit, while an insect's head is separated from the thorax, or middle body, unit. Spiders have no antennae, while insects do. Spiders have no wings, while many (but not all) insects do. Spiders do not have stingers.

By scientific classification (or taxonomy), spiders and insects are both arthropods: invertebrate animals with external skeletons, segmented bodies, and jointed legs. Lobsters, shrimp, and centipedes are also arthropods. Spiders are in the class of arthropods called Arachnida; insects are in the class Insecta. So spiders and insects are related to each other in about the same way humans and fish are related: humans and fish are vertebrate animals (having internal skeletons).

Spiders make up the order Araneae in the class Arachnida. Their Arachnida cousins are mites and ticks (in the order Acari); scorpions (order Scorpionida); and harvestmen, commonly called daddy long-legs (order Opiliones), among others. These all have eight legs and two-section bodies, but differ from spiders in a variety

Simplified Taxonomic Categories

Phylum: Arthropoda

Class: Arachnida

Order: Araneae

Infraorder: Araneomorphae

*Family:

Agelenidae (grass spiders)

Amaurobiidae (hacked mesh weavers)

Araneidae (orbweavers)

Clubionidae (sac spiders)

Corinnidae (antmimic spiders)

Dictynidae (meshweavers)

Gnaphosidae (ground spiders)

Hahniidae (combtailed spiders)

Linyphiidae (sheetweb weavers)

Lycosidae (wolf spiders)

Philodromidae (running crab spiders)

Pholcidae (cellar spiders)

Pisauridae (nursery web spiders)

Salticidae (jumping spiders)

Tetragnathidae (longjawed orbweavers)

Theridiidae (cobweb weavers)

Thomisidae (crab spiders)

*List includes only spider families detailed in this book.

A grass spider.

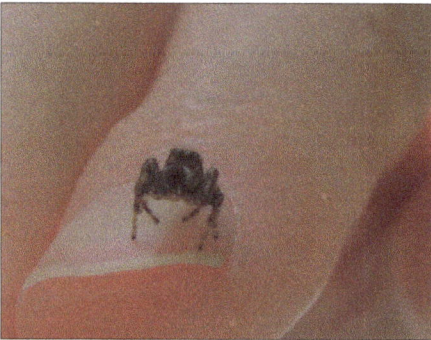

A jumping spider.

A deer tick.

of ways. (Harvestmen look like they're all head because the two parts appear joined seamlessly, though they aren't really.) These other arachnids make minimal or no use of silk, lack the spiders' spinneret mechanisms on the abdomen that disperse it, and do not deliver their venom through bites the way spiders do. That's if they even have venom, which daddy long-legs, for example, do not.

Spiders have lived on Earth for about 300 million years. Few spider fossils have been found from before about 65 million years ago, but an arthropod very much like a spider, called *Attercopus fimbriungis*, with silk-producing spigots, lived in North America during the Devonian period, roughly 370 million years ago. By about 300 million years ago, primitive spiders in the order Mesothelae seem to have been well-established, and spiders survived the huge Permian-Triassic extinction event of 252 million years ago in which up to 95 percent of all known life forms were wiped out. Orb webs began to appear in the following Triassic period. Spiders fared durably again about 65 million years ago in the Cretaceous-Tertiary extinction event, when an asteroid about six miles wide slammed into the Earth in the vicinity of the Gulf of Mexico, altered the climate, and wiped out 75 percent of all living species, including the dinosaurs.

The *World Spider Catalog* in 2020 listed more than 48,400 species of spiders identified and validated. Arachnologists estimate there are at least 75,000 species, and possibly as many as 190,000 species of spiders presently on the planet. About 680 species of spiders are thought to live within the North American region we call Maine.

2. SPIDER BIOLOGY

To understand spiders, it's helpful to be able to spot and name a few of their body parts.

The eight legs extend from the spider's cephalothorax, and have a variety of resting postures. The legs can stretch out in front and back of the spider, as nursery web spiders do at rest, or the front legs can bow to the sides, as crab spiders' do. Some spiders at rest fold up their legs and pull them in underneath.

The spider's mouth is at the very front of its face, and has two "jaws" called chelicerae. In spiders of the infraorder Araneomorphae, which comprises 96 percent of all spiders, the chelicerae are arranged so they move side to side (or diaxially); all spiders indigenous to Maine are araneomorphs. The other 4 percent of spider species are in the infraorder Mygalomorphae, and have chelicerae that close horizontally and strike downward (or paraxially); an example of a mygalomorph is the tarantula, which comes to Maine only by accident or as a pet. On the tips of the chelicerae are fangs, often with serrated edges too small to see easily without a magnifying glass or microscope. Near the tip of the fang is a tiny opening through which venom is injected into prey when the spider bites. The fangs of most spiders are so small that they normally can't break human skin.

There are two appendages beside the mouth, called pedipalps, or just palps, which act almost like little hands and serve a variety of purposes, including in eating, cleaning, and copulation.

On the head, the exoskeleton covering the front region of the cephalothorax is called the carapace. Along its front, sides, and top are the spider's eyes. Most spider species have eight eyes; some have six eyes, a very few have four or only two eyes, and a small number of species, mostly cave dwellers, have no eyes.

Most spiders don't see very well, compared to humans and birds, for example. But some spiders that hunt for their food, such as wolf spiders and jumping spiders, have relatively sharp vision.

Spiders' heads and abdomens take a great range of shapes, sizes, and markings. In some, like the common house spider (family Theridiidae), the abdomen is much larger than the head. In many species of long-jawed orbweavers (family Tetragnathidae), the head and abdomen are often long and narrow by comparison.

Brian Friedmann examines an orb web with his magnifier in Steuben, Maine.

3. IDENTIFYING SPIDERS

Identifying an individual spider to its species is for the most part difficult to impossible, in many cases, without a microscope and a familiarity with spider anatomy. Even the photos in guidebooks are sometimes unhelpful because spiders of the same species can differ significantly in overall appearance, not to mention that females are usually larger than males and often differ from males in overall appearance. But there are some prominent clues to a spider's family and genus observable by eye, and a few spiders common in Maine, New England, and eastern Canada can be recognized on sight by backyard naturalists with a little practice.

It's helpful when out spidering to carry around a 10-15x hand lens (best used when held very close to your eye) and a small vial or two with which you can capture a spider, look at it up close, and then release it or put it in a dish with alcohol and observe it under a microscope. Some anatomical parts you can usually see with your naked eye can help narrow down the identification:

Body shape and coloration. The spiders in Maine come in all sizes from tiny hackledmesh weavers barely a millimeter or so in total body length up to large orbweavers like the barn spider that can be 22 mm (about an inch) in total body length and even larger. Look for the color of the spider, the size and shape of the abdomen, and any markings, the more ornate of which on the abdomen is called a folium (for example, on the bridge orbweaver). Some orbweaving spiders have humps of more and less prominence where you might envision their shoulders to be (for example, the barn spider). Some spiders have symmetrical spots (for example, the six-spotted orbweaver).

Spinnerets. The spinnerets are the organs on the back of the spider's abdomen that extrude silk. In some spiders the spinnerets are not readily visible to your casual eye, but in others they are. If your spider has two or more prominent, cylinder-shaped spinnerets, you probably have a ground spider (family Gnaphosidae; for example, the parson spider). If your spider's spinnerets are still obvious but seem stubbier and more conical-shaped, then you might have a sac spider. Remember, the spinnerets spin silk—they are not stingers. The long protrusions on the abdomens of *Agelenopsis* grass spiders, for example, look at a glance like stingers, but they're not—they're spinnerets.

Eyes. Virtually all the spiders in Maine have eight eyes, though a few species have six eyes. The eyes are arranged in patterns that usually make up curved or straight rows on the carapace. It takes some practice to get familiar with eye patterns, but easily recognizable are the eyes of jumping spiders (family Salti-

A jumping spider.

A wolf spider (*Schizocosa* genus).

cidae), whose two main eyes are quite large and peer forward so directly they really seem to be looking at you. Wolf spiders (family Lycosidae) also have two large eyes set over a row of four smaller eyes above the mouth, with two more eyes (which may at first seem more like dark flecks than eyes) flanking the large eyes farther back. A chart of the eye rows can help determine the family of your spider. No chart is provided in this book, but helpful ones are available in guidebooks and reliable websites.

Palps. The palps, or pedipalps, are the two little handlike appendages in front of the spider's mouth. In general, it's possible to tell a female spider from a male spider by the size of the palps: the male's palps are noticeably larger and more swollen than the female's. The palps are used to handle silk, prey items, and in some species egg sacs, or to clean mouth parts after a meal. In male spiders the palps are the external sex organs used to transfer sperm to the female's epigynum, which is located underneath her abdomen.

Legs. Many spider species have characteristic ways of holding their eight legs. Crab spiders (family Thomisidae) and running crab spiders (family Philodromidae) hold their front legs roughly the same way sea crabs do. Nursery web spiders when at rest hold their long front legs out in front and often stretch their long back legs out behind. A spider's legs may have noticeably long spines, or spines may be absent. Some spiders' legs are a solid dark or light color, as on some jumping spiders, while others' are distinctly banded, as on some fishing spiders.

4. SPIDERS IN MAINE

The science of arachnology developed largely in Europe during the 19th century and reached its first milestone, in a way, with the publication of Eugene Simon's *Histoire Naturelle des Araignées* from 1892 to 1903, which provided an outline for spider classifications that arachnologists have built on since then.

In the United States, early spider studies were often done in association with general surveys of other animals. In Maine during the late 1800s and early 1900s, a handful of naturalists such as James H. Emerton, Elizabeth B. Bryant, and Irving H. Blake collected spiders during their forays to the state inventorying insects. The first cumulative list of spiders in Maine was published in 1946 by William Procter, in his *Biological Survey of the Mount Desert Region*, following his inventory of invertebrates there in the 1920s, '30s, and '40s. It remained the most comprehensive list of spiders in Maine for decades, until the scientific study, collection, and cataloging of spiders in Maine picked up in the 1970s and '80s, especially under the efforts of Daniel Jennings, Maine's foremost spider expert around the turn of the 21st century. Jennings, with the help of a variety of specialists, has made and published inventories of spiders from Mount Katahdin and the Moosehorn Wildlife Refuge in Washington County; studied spiders in clear-cut, spruce, and blueberry field ranges in Somerset, Piscataquis, Aroostook, and Washington Counties; and studied predation of spiders on spruce budworm moths in central and eastern Maine, as well as spiders' use of lepidopteran shelters at sites in Bangor and Old Town, among many other projects.

The definitive published catalog of spiders in Maine is *Spiders (Arachnida: Araneae) of Milbridge, Washington County, Maine* by Jennings and Frank Graham, Jr., published in 2007 following their study made from 1991 to 2005. A more comprehensive, statewide list of authenticated sightings, "Preliminary checklist of Maine spiders," has been compiled by Jennings with help from former Maine state entomologist Charlene Donahue and the Maine Forest Service; that list was expected to be published later in 2020. In recent years a number of arachnologists have made extensive studies of invasive linyphiids and theridiids in Down East Maine.

What spiders might you be most likely to spot in Maine? Daniel Jennings told me in a phone conversation a few years ago that they might be *Pardosa*, a genus of wolf spiders, who live mainly in fields or dry sandy areas, or you might

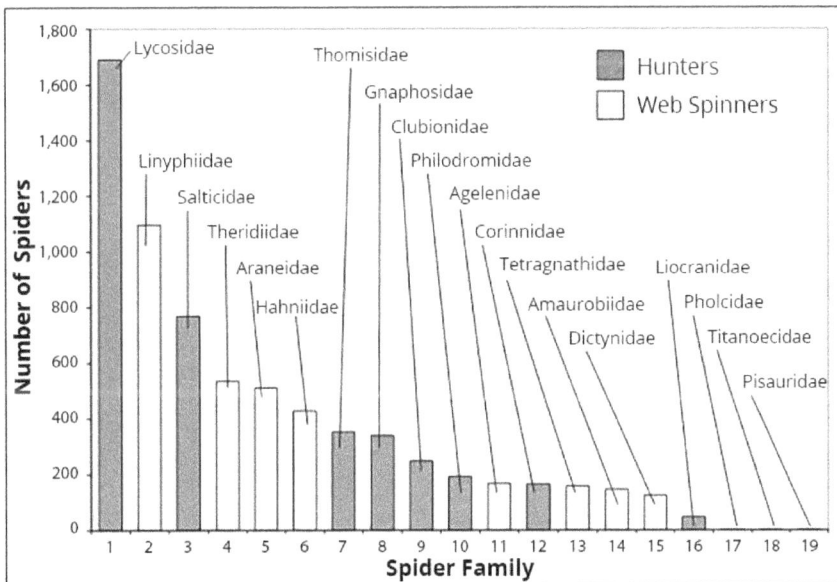

Rank-order abundances of spider families collected in Milbridge, Washington County, Maine, during the period 1991 – 2005. (*Source: Spiders (Arachnida: Araneae) of Milbridge, Washington County, Maine*)

see in your kitchen the parson spider (*Herpyllus ecclesiasticus*), which is a ground spider that sometimes ventures indoors. But it depends on where you are. There are coastal spiders and woods spiders, garden spiders and house. Where I live in central Maine, I often see black-and-yellow garden spiders (*Argiope aurantia*) and banded garden spiders (*Argiope trifasciata*), partly because they're abundant in the fields I trek regularly and also because they're relatively easy to spot hanging in their orb webs in brush and grass. Inside my house I often see common house spiders (*Parasteatoda*), which are cobweb weavers. Tiny, barely noticed spiders like some jumping spiders (family Salticidae) might outnumber larger, more conspicuous spiders like the *Argiope* and nursery web spiders (family Pisauridae) whose bodies can be a half inch or more long.

About 680 species of spiders are thought to live within the North American region we call Maine, roughly the same number as are found in the whole of the United Kingdom. In their Milbridge study, Jennings and Graham collected spiders from 302 species; the web spinning species collected outnumbered the hunting species. The most abundant spider family in the Milbridge study were wolf spiders (family Lycosidae), followed by sheetweb weavers (family Linyphiidae) and jumping spiders (family Salticidae), along with 16 other families. Within the families are species literally too numerous to name so far, and within the species, of course, are millions of individuals. The British naturalist W.S. Bristowe in the 1950s estimated about 2 million spiders inhabited each acre of his farmland. Jennings told me this did not seem like an unrealistic number for Maine, either.

Spiders are one of nature's most versatile, durable creatures with such an incredible array of lifestyles, habits, and approaches to making a living that generalizations about what spiders do or don't do are rarely true of all of them. Each family, genus, and species has its own unique, and incredible life story. Following are some facts about spiders found in the vicinity of Maine (as well as a few that are not usually found here) that hopefully you will find interesting. I, for one, am profoundly fascinated by them.

5. SCOPE AND ARRANGEMENT OF THIS BOOK

This book focuses on spiders likely to be spotted in Maine; it is by no means comprehensive. Its principal local reference source is Jennings and Graham's *Spiders (Arachnida: Araneae) of Milbridge, Maine*. Spiders of course are unconcerned with human political boundaries, and as indicated by the title of Jennings and Donahue's "Preliminary checklist of Maine spiders (Arachnida: Araneae), including species found elsewhere in New England and in Atlantic Canada," this book should also be of interest to readers in the Northeastern states as well as New Brunswick, Nova Scotia, and Québec.

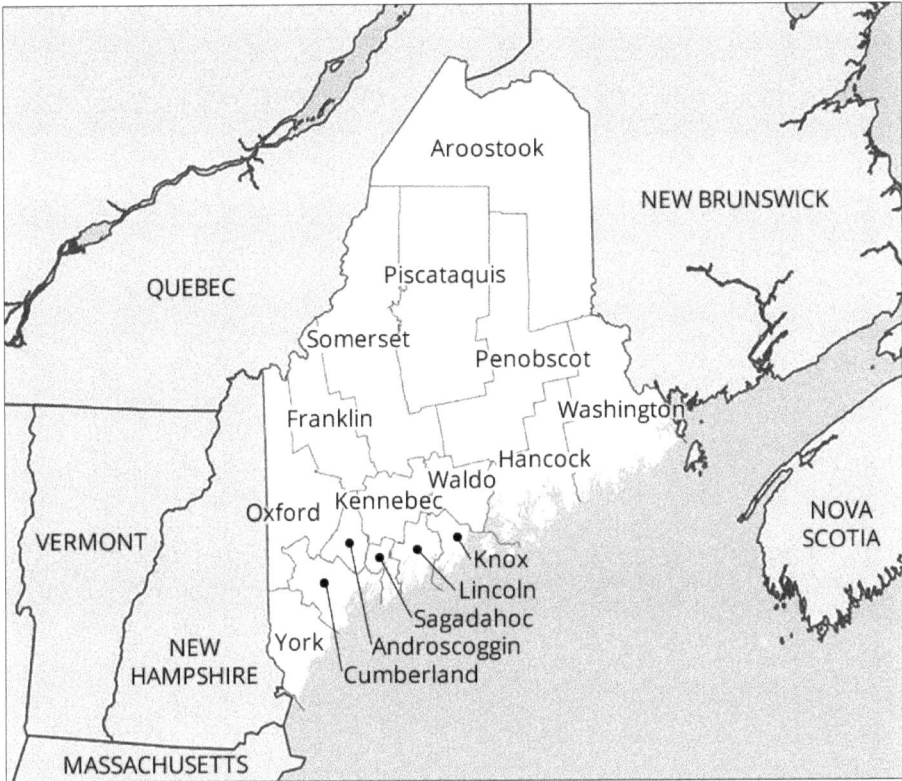

The geographic area where spiders covered in this book are commonly found. Many of them are found in other areas of North America, as well.

This book has two main components: 1. a catalog, or list of spiders with notes of interest and photographs, and 2. short sidebar pieces on interesting aspects of spiders set into gray boxes among the catalog entries.

The catalog is divided into two sections: hunting spiders and web-spinning spiders. Within each section, spiders are listed in alphabetical order by family name (Agelenidae, Amaurobiidae, Araneidae, Dictynidae, and so on), and under each family section are examples of genus and species, given in alphabetical order by scientific name.

The sidebars offer short essays and factual rehearsals on topics such as eating, mating, ballooning, silk, and others.

Finally, a list of works consulted is provided to indicate the many places where information was gleaned. Full, formal scientific citation style is not employed, but enough information is provided for interested readers to easily find each work and, for the curious, the sources of details.

A Catalog of Spiders
in Maine

A male grass spider.

Web Spinners

GRASS SPIDERS, OR FUNNEL WEAVERS
Family Agelenidae

Grass spiders, or funnel weavers, are medium-sized spiders, often brown or gray, with long spinnerets on the back of the abdomen. They can be distinguished from wolf spiders by their longer spinnerets and by the eyes arranged in basically two curved rows on the front of the spider's face.

Grass spiders build the round, flat webs you see scattered around the lawn in the morning when dew is fresh on the silk, and sometimes in other places such as the side of the house. They fashion a funnel near the center of the web, where they sit and sometimes peek out as they wait for prey. When a bug ambles onto the web, which is not sticky, the grass spider senses the vibration and rushes out to capture the bug and take it back into the retreat.

Identifying an agelenid to species, and even to genus, is difficult and often impossible without a microscope to examine its body parts.

Grass spiders are pretty commonly seen in central Maine. They're abundant in our lawn all summer, and I've found them on the kitchen counter and in the bathtub, where females sometimes have wandered in the house to overwinter and live a second summer. Egg sacs are generally prepared in late fall or early spring, and the spiders reach adulthood by August or September. Males tend to die before winter, but some may overwinter indoors, while others enter dia-

Grass spiders in their funnel webs.

pause, the arachnid version of hibernation, as adults or juveniles in silk retreats under rocks.

The *World Spider Catalog* in 2019 listed more than 1,300 species of funnel weavers worldwide, and they're one of the most numerous families of spiders in North America. Jennings and Graham collected about 200 individuals in four species in their Milbridge study, the 11th most abundant of 19 families collected in the study. In a study of strips of clear-cut land in Piscataquis County made by Jennings in the late 1970s, grass spiders were the second most numerous family collected, with wolf spiders (Lycosidae) the most numerous, followed by hackledmesh weavers (Amaurobiidae), and a subfamily of sheetweb weavers (Linyphiinae).

The hobo spider (*Eratigena agrestis*, formerly *Tegenaria agrestis*) is listed on the University of Maine Cooperative Extension's website as "rarely found in Maine"; in the summer of 2019 a pest control worker photographed a large spider in Burnham which appeared to be a hobo spider. Also known as the aggressive house spider, the hobo spider is rumored to administer a nasty bite causing a necrotic lesion in humans; but researchers investigating this claim have found no evidence that hobo spider bites are medically significant (or that hobo spiders are particularly aggressive—the word *agrestis* means "of the fields," not "aggressive"). Hobo spiders were introduced to northwestern North America from Europe, and get their name from lore that they're prone to hitching rides to other ranges. Their cousin, the barn funnel weaver (*Tegenaria domestica*) does occur in Maine, but is not known to bite people.

Cameron says the word agelenid may come from the 19th century naturalist Charles Walckenaer's conflation of the goddess Athena's epithet Αγελευ (Age-lei) with her name (Αθηνα) to create the genus name *Agelena*. This would be the only spider name that alludes specifically to Athena, who became piqued at Arachne's pride in her weaving skills and engaged her in a contest. Despite Arachne's hubris, Athena found her so good at weaving that she punished her by turning her into a spider, rather than killing her.

A male grass spider (*Coras*) on the living room carpet.

Grass spider (*Agelenopsis*)

Agelenopsis genus grass spiders are the ones peeking out of the funnel webs on the lawn. The different species are so similar in overall appearance that normally it's not possible to distinguish them without a microscope to examine their genital organs. *Agelenopsis naevia* tends to be the largest of the genus. Jennings and Graham's Milbridge study identified only three species, *A. actuosa*, *A. potteri*, and *A. putabana*.

The males of some species of *Agelenopsis* have a very unusual courtship practice. The male cautiously approaches a female through vibratory signaling, which is common among spiders. But when the female finally allows him to mount her, he begins stroking the sides of her abdomen with his legs, and the female soon curls up her legs and enters a cataleptic-like state. He then uses his chelicerae, or jaws, to gently grasp one of her legs and turn her on her side in position to copulate. Researchers believe the passive state may be induced by a chemical spray emitted by the male.

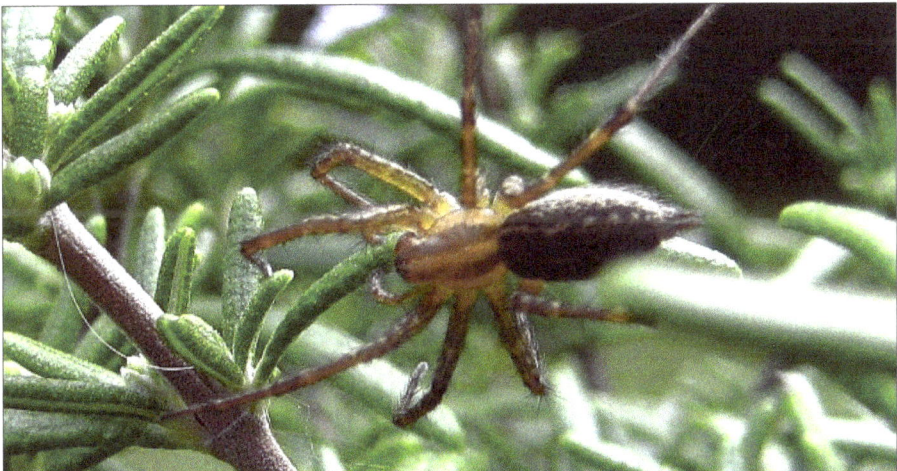

A grass spider (*Agelenopsis naevia*).

Coras medicinalis

Coras medicinalis, aka the medicine spider, is found under loose bark and in hollow tree stumps, as well as in houses, usually cellars, where it weaves its funnel web in corners—although the individual pictured here was first spotted making its way along my wife Bonnie's shirt. Adults and juveniles overwinter by entering diapause, the arachnid version of hibernation, in silk retreats.

The naturalist N.M. Hentz first named this spider *Tegenaria medicinalis* in the early 19th century, observing in a professional note that its web "possesses very narcotic powers, and it has been administered apparently with success in some cases of fevers." *Coras medicinalis* silk is not used in that way nowadays, as far as I know. The genus name *Coras* is taken from a minor character in Virgil's *Aeneid* whose epithet is "eager Coras," according to Cameron.

This medicine spider (*Coras medicinalis*) was captured lumbering along a person's shoulder.

speaker / spell

kolusu

komutewestu

kotuwewestu

s/he speaks

s/he spea

s/he wa

speech

"Amushopik" wanders across a page of the University of Maine Press's *Passamaquoddy-Maliseet Dictionary*. The spider is probably a young cobweb weaver.

Spider Names

Spiders, like most animals, have a sort of matrix of names. Each spider family has a scientific name and a common name; and each documented spider species has a scientific name, and many (but not all) species have their own common names. Spiders also are referred to by their predatory practices: hunters and web spinners.

So for example, the common name of the large, conspicuous black and yellow spider sitting in her web in a willow herb thicket or under a windowframe is the black-and-yellow garden spider. Her scientific name is *Argiope aurantia* (*Argiope* is the genus name; *aurantia* is the species name). *Argiope aurantia* is in the family Araneidae, whose common name is the orbweavers. And so this spider may be called a black-and-yellow garden spider; *Argiope aurantia*; an araneid; an orbweaver; or a web spinning spider. All are correct, usable names for the same spider.

For another example, the common name of a spider that is widespread in Maine is the thin-legged wolf spider. The scientific name of the species that might be the most abundant is *Pardosa moesta*. It is in the family Lycosidae, whose common name is the wolf spiders, who are hunters. And so this spider may accurately be called a thin-legged wolf spider; *Pardosa moesta*; a lycosid; a wolf spider; or a hunting spider. Since there are at least 16 different species within the genus *Pardosa* and they're almost impossible to tell apart without close anatomical inspection, when a naturalist with a practiced eye spots one in the field, it gets called simply *Pardosa*.

Arachne

The ancient Greek word αραχνη (arachne, "spider") is the progenitor of our words arachnid, arachnology (the study of spiders and other arachnids), and Arachnida (the taxonomic class). The first century Latin poet Ovid tells in his *Metamorphoses* the story of Arachne, a weaver whose skill was so great it got the attention of the goddess Athena. One of Athena's many technical competencies was spinning and weaving. Disgruntled by Arachne's challenge to the supremacy of her spinning skill, Athena disguised herself as an old woman and suggested to Arachne that she ask the goddess to forgive her for thinking too much of her work. Arachne bristled and wondered why Athena didn't come to say this herself, whereupon Athena dropped her disguise and challenged Arachne to a weaving contest.

They set to work creating cloths with intricate designs depicting the lives of the gods, and Arachne's stories were none too flattering. But when they finished, her work was so skillful that Athena couldn't find any fault with it. Incensed, she tore up Arachne's tapestry and hit her on the head. Arachne then felt so disgraced before the goddess that she slipped a noose around her neck to hang herself. Athena, with a range of emotions unavailable to many of the other gods, pitied Arachne and lifted her up while she hung. She then decreed that Arachne and her descendants would from that time forward dangle in punishment for her hubris. Using the juice of Hecate's herb, Athena turned Arachne into a spider. Her spinning skills remained.

The Greek word arachne likely had an earlier form *αρακονα (araksna), which is cognate with a likely early Latin word *araksneyā, which led to the classical Latin word araneus (and aranea, which in Ovid's time meant specifically spider web). The Latin word gained use in scientific nomenclature developed during the 18th and 19th centuries. So now we have the taxonomic class Arachnida (invertebrate animals with eight legs, no wings, and no antennae); the order Araneae (spiders); the family Araneidae (orbweavers); and the genus *Araneus* for a group of anatomically related orbweavers. (By convention in zoology, family names end with the suffix -idae, which is the plural form of the Latin suffix -id (derived from Greek -idēs) indicating patronymic lineage; in Greek mythology, Agamemnon was a son of Atreus, hence a member of the House of Atreides. Spider family names follow this convention: Lycosidae, Salticidae, Theridiidae.)

H.D. Cameron's "An etymological dictionary of North American spider genus names" (Chapter 75 of Ubick, et al., *Spiders of North America*) indicates that as a general trend, the early naturalists often had no literal or metaphorical connections in mind when they selected scientific names for spiders. A lot of scientific names are surprisingly arbitrary, fanciful, and even random. Early naturalists such as Pierre André Latreille, Charles Walckenaer, and C.L. Koch often just cast about for a workable word. Since their academic background emphasized the importance of

Greek and Latin history, language, and culture in ways that have all but vanished nowadays, they mined Greek and Latin lexicons and mythologies for names that gave authoritative weight to their descriptions. Sometimes they adapted words that had historical connections to spider studies, such as τετραγναθοσ (tetragnathos, "four-jawed")—a word used as early as the first century B.C.—to make the name *Tetragnatha* (aka long-jawed orbweavers). Sometimes they grabbed a word from, for example, a book of mythology, such as the name Meta, an obscure figure from Greek myth, to mark a genus of tetragnathid (e.g., *Meta ovalis*, aka the cave orbweaver). Sometimes they pieced together names from grammatical forms of different words, such as the genus name *Amaurobius*, which Koch created from the Greek αμαυροσ (amauros, "dark") and a combining form -βιοσ (-bios, "living"). And sometimes they got fanciful: Latreille assigned the genus name *Pachygnatha* in part because he liked the rhyme with *Tetragnatha*. From time to time taxonomists come upon a spider name whose origin is a complete puzzle, but since it may still be in use unofficially, in catalogs it is given the zoological label "nomen dubium" (doubtful name); an example of this in the *World Spider Catalog* is *Schizocosa algerica*, which somehow became a replacement name for the 19th century name *Lycosa erratica*.

Even now, as new spider species are discovered and new names are assigned, the coining of the names isn't terribly systematic. The cable television comedian Stephen Colbert cajoled for a spider to be named after him and succeeded—in 2008 arachnologists named a newly identified species of trapdoor spider *Aptostichus stephencolberti*. Maine's premier spider expert of the late 20th and early 21st centuries, Daniel Jennings, has two species named for him: the cobweb weaver *Chrosiothes jenningsi*, that he discovered in West Virginia, and a subspecies of running crab spider, *Philodromus rufus jenningsi*, that was discovered in Kansas.

"Spider"

The European languages that grew from Latin name spiders after the arachne-araneus thread: in Spanish a spider is araña; in Italian, ragno; in French, araignée. English, though, is a Germanic language, and our word first appears in its present form in the mid-1400s as Spyder, a new pronunciation of the Middle English word spithre, from Chaucer's time in the mid-1300s. That word is the post-1066 (when the French-speaking Normans invaded Britain) version of the Old English word spiþra (Spithra), which etymologists believe was preceded by the older proto-Germanic words *spenthro and *spenwanan meaning "to spin." The modern German word for spider is Spinne; Swedish, Spindel. So by etymology, deep inside our word spider is spin—a spider is a spinner.

In Old English, the word gangewifre, meaning something like "a weaver as he goes," was apparently used for spiders. There is also an Old English word wæterbucca, which one lexicon gives as meaning water-spider and by pronunciation puts one in mind of the word water-bug. It turns out the word bug may come from the Welsh word bwg, meaning specter or ghost.

More common in Old English (roughly, pre-1066) is the word âtorcoppe (attercoppe), meaning poison spider. It may have formed from the words attor (poison or venom) and coppe (meaning top, or possibly head). There is also an Old English construction âtor-loppe, which is translated literally as spinner of a web; loppe can mean spider, flea, or silkworm, probably in association with the sense of dangling.

The words coppe and attor are spread deep in etymologic history. A Welsh word for spider is copyn. Coppe is cognate with other northern European words for spider such as Flemish coppe, Dutch spinnecop, and Danish edderkop. Attor is cognate with an old German word eittar, whose probable forerunner in proto-Germanic was the affix *aitra-, meaning poisonous ulcer, which in turn is cognate with Greek oîdos, meaning a swelling—which probably goes back to an original Indo-European affix, *oid-.

This connection of spiders to swellings in Indo-European languages makes a strange coincidence with certain words used in Algonquian languages in North America. The Passamaquoddy-Maliseet peoples of far eastern Maine and New Brunswick call a spider amushopik, a homonym also meaning a cancerous tumor. The Mi'gmaq people of northern Maine, New Brunswick, and Québec refer to a spider as go'gwejij, also a homonym for a cancerous tumor.

In Passamaquoddy-Maliseet, a cobweb or spider's silk is amushopihkewi-ahpap. In Mi'gmaq a spider web is go'gwejijua'pi. Another dictionary indicates "Micmacs" farther east in Canada used a similar word, owöějit. The Penobscots of north-central and coastal Maine have the word mamselabika for spider in their Eastern Abenaki version of the Algonquian languages. Western Abenaki has, similarly, the word mamsahlabika, "he makes many nets," according to one dictionary, and for spider webs, mamsahlabipikonal, meaning literally "very many net strings."

Up here in the 21st century, the best way to find a spider's accepted scientific name is to consult the *World Spider Catalog* (https://wsc.nmbe.ch/) of The World Spider Catalog Association. For officially accepted common names, see the American Arachnological Society's publication *Common Names of Arachnids*.

And by the way, a group of spiders is a gaggle. ✳

A hackledmesh weaver (*Callobius*) on the kitchen counter.

HACKLEDMESH WEAVERS
Family Amaurobiidae

Hackledmesh weavers are medium-sized, usually brown or black spiders who live in a messy-looking web with a tubular retreat, similar to the retreat of grass spiders except that the hackledmesh weaver's web is not typically flat. It tends to feature threads radiating from the entrance, which the spider monitors for vibrations. They build their webs under bark, in trees, and on walls in or outside the house.

Part of the reason the web is messy looking is that amaurobiids are cribellate spiders. This means they have a platelike organ called a cribellum that spins out silk. Silk spun through the cribellum is then carded or combed by a series of curved bristles, called a calamistrum, on their fourth legs, giving it a somewhat ragged appearance. Most spiders are ecribellate; that is, most do not have a cribellum.

Hackledmesh weavers tend to live on the ground among rocks and crevices. I see *Amaurobius ferox* and *Callobius* species around my house in Troy at all times of the year. They are known to get inside the house on firewood. The hackledmesh weavers generally live through the winter, the males as juveniles who reach adulthood the next spring and die after mating. Females are thought to live at least two years.

25

A hackledmesh weaver in the very last stage of his molt, in the kitchen sink.

Amaurobiids are one of the few spiders who do not get panicked by predatory wasps. The blue-black spider wasps that we have in Maine prowl the ground for spiders. When a female catches one, she paralyzes it with a sting, drags it back to the nest, lays an egg on it, and covers it over for the wasp larva to eat after hatching. Most spiders understandably flee these wasps, but studies show that some species of hackledmesh weavers can overpower and eat the predator.

The *World Spider Catalog* in 2019 listed 276 species of hackledmesh weavers worldwide, with 71 species north of Mexico. Jennings and Graham identified just under 200 hackledmesh weavers in their Milbridge study, making it the 14th most abundant family collected, out of 19 categories. They were among the most abundant spider families found in Jennings' study of clear-cut land in Piscataquis County in the late 1970s. (Wolf spiders were the most abundant in the study, followed by a subfamily of sheetweb weavers, hackledmesh weavers, and grass spiders.) Amaurobiidae is one of the spider families that has undergone considerable revision in recent decades, with spiders moved in and out of the family as taxonomic criteria are refined.

Amaurobiidae is a strange word which means, roughly, living in the dark. The name for the genus *Amaurobius* was made from the Greek αμαυροσ (amauros, "dark") and a combining form -βιοσ (bios, "living") by the 19th century naturalist C.L. Koch.

Amaurobius ferox

Amaurobius ferox is a medium-sized to large brown or light brown spider, sometimes with lighter chevronlike markings on the back, and with large, shiny chelicerae, or mouth parts. This spider was introduced to North America from Europe, but resembles its native cousin, *Amaurobius borealis*, which is also found in Maine and turned up fairly abundantly in Jennings and Graham's Milbridge study. *Amaurobius ferox*'s life cycle includes matriphagy, in which the spiderlings eat their mother.

A juvenile hackledmesh weaver (*Amaurobius ferox*).

27

Callobius bennetti

Callobius resembles *A. ferox* in overall appearance, with bulging chelicerae, or mouth parts, but tends to be a little smaller and darker colored. It lives on the ground under logs, rocks, and debris, and has been found on the carpet and kitchen counter in our house. The web usually is built mostly under cover, which can include a crevice in a wall. Jennings and Graham found a good many individuals of *C. bennetti* in their Milbridge study.

According to Cameron, the genus name *Callobius* was invented as a rhyme with the genus names *Callioplus* (the tangled nest spider, an amaurobiid now officially known as *Cybaeopsis*) and *Amaurobius*. Callio- is derived from the Greek καλλοσ (kallos, "beauty"), as in the word καλλιοπλια (kallioplia, "possession of fine armor"—perhaps referring, Cameron speculates, to an enlargement on the male pedipalp resembling a weapon).

Callobius bennetti in the woodpile.

An early morning orb web in Steuben, Maine.

Webs and Silk

One of the most beautiful of nature's phenomena is a spider's orb web. Its engineering parameters are precise almost beyond belief, with fearfully perfect symmetry. It inspires aesthetic responses in more layers than it has radii, from joy in beauty, to admiration of craftsmanship, to delicacy, to senses of universal scale, to the moral irony of its violent purpose. Orb webs are such exquisite masterpieces that you, or I at least, cannot help but wonder about the state and quality of intelligence underlying them.

Orb webs are, to use Robert Frost's word, designed. Their main purpose is to capture prey, and they also play roles in courtship, heat regulation, and defense against predators. They're constructed more or less vertically to the ground, sometimes at slight angles according to the species of the builder. Orbweavers (aka araneids), such as the garden spiders, generally weave fairly tight spirals with a closed center that in some species includes a heavy squiggle of silk called a stabilimentum, whose purpose is not clear. The webs of tetragnathids, or long-jawed orbweavers, on the other hand, tend to be inclined at an angle to vertical, have fewer radii than araneid webs, and are usually open in the center.

Orbweavers set up the construction site by trailing a strand of silk from some prominent spot such as a timothy tip into the breeze, which catches the strand and tacks it to a distant leaf or other solid surface. The spider then hustles back and forth paying out silk along this bridge. When the bridge is sturdy enough, the spider ties on another line and drops down to secure it on a stalk be-

A linyphiid underneath her sheetweb.

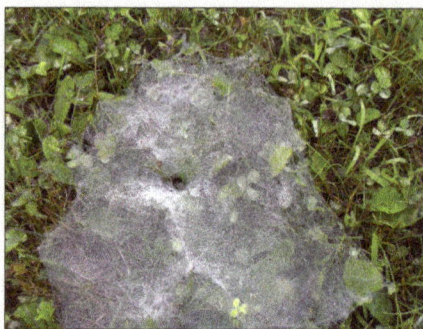

A grass spider and its funnel web.

A bowl-and-doily web, spun by a bowl-and-doily spider (*Frontinella communis*) in Steuben, Maine.

A house spider in her cobweb.

low. This is the first frame.

Next the spider constructs radial spokes and two sets of spirals—one a scaffolding that will be taken down at the end of the construction project, and the other the permanent structure that will snare flies, mosquitoes, butterflies, and whatever else wanders in. A black-and-yellow garden spider (*Argiope aurantia*) takes about a half-hour to an hour to complete the engineering of an orb web 1 to 2 feet in diameter.

Some orbweavers take down their web in the morning and build a new web every night. In an after-dark spi-

dering expedition one summer, some fellow spidercatchers and I were puzzled to observe several araneids trying to disassemble their webs; soon we realized the spiders were fooled by our headlamps into thinking daylight had come. In some species, taking the web down involves eating the silk, whose proteins take about 45 minutes to get processed through the spider's system and ready to be respun into new silk.

Orb webs stand out to us partly because of their beauty and partly because they're just conspicuous. But other kinds of capture webs are

Dragline silk on a mossy ledge in Steuben, Maine.

equally intricate: sheetwebs, funnel webs, and cobwebs, also called space-filling webs. Sheetwebs made by linyphiids (sheetweb weavers) consist, in general, of a sheet of silk, with modifications such as a convex sheet with a silk dome overhead, from which they run vertical threads to knock flying prey down onto the sheet. Most sheetweb weavers don't build a retreat into the web. Instead, the spider hangs upside down underneath the sheet and, when the insect falls, cuts a hole in the sheet and pulls the prey down through.

Grass spiders (family Agelenidae) make the flat webs you see covered in dew on the lawn in the morning. A funnel is built into the web, where the spider waits. When it senses vibrations made in the silk by an entangled bug, it runs out to capture the meal.

Hackledmesh weavers (family Amaurobiidae) also build funnel webs, but most of the web is made up of the funnel, or retreat, with lines of silk running out from the opening to entangle bugs that wander by.

Cobweb weavers (family Theridiidae), such as the common house spider (*Parasteatoda*), build what look like disorganized three-dimensional tangles, though studies show the construction of the tangle is a fairly systematic process. Meshweavers (family Dictynidae) also build space-filling webs, often in the tops of plants like goldenrod that have gone to seed. Their space-filling web has a particularly unkempt look because, like hackledmesh weavers, the dictynids are cribellate spiders, meaning they have an organ called a cribellum, which helps produce extremely fine strands of silk. The

A jumping spider in the process of constructing a silk retreat while captive in a vial.

strands are extruded through spinnerets, as in all spiders, combined, and then combed with a toothed organ on their hind legs called a calamistrum. The result is a tangle of fluffy, unkempt-looking silk.

Silk for many purposes

Not all spiders build capture webs. Wolf spiders, ground spiders, and jumping spiders, for example, are hunters and don't use snares. But they all make silk for other purposes. Depending on its needs, a spider may have as many as seven different silk glands to make different types of silk. There are special silks for egg sacs and for wrapping prey. Dragline silk can serve a number of purposes, including maintaining a jumping spi-

der's orientation to its surroundings and providing attractive scents to prospective mates. A jumping spider held in a vial is apt to spin a retreat to hide in. Spiders that construct capture webs also produce specialized silks for joining lines, for making safety and frame lines, and for non-sticky threads used in web scaffolding.

Spider silk is famously very tough. Abandoned cobweb silk can remain intact in basement ceilings for years, partly because of its resistance to bacterial decay. Spider silk in general has about half the tensile strength of steel. (Tensile strength is a measure of the stress a length can withstand before tearing under its own weight.) A typical dragline can be nearly 50 miles long before it breaks under its own weight, which is longer than the breaking point of a length of steel of the same hairlike width, because the silk is less dense and weighs less than the length of steel.

Silks also have extraordinary elasticity, meaning the ability to stretch and then return to a resting shape. The huge webs of golden silk orbweavers (*Nephila* genus) in the tropics have been used for fishing nets, and the silk also has been used to make clothing, including a vestment made entirely of the gold-colored silk presented to the pope. Some silks can take up to seven to 10 times more energy to fracture than an equivalent volume of Kevlar, a material used in bullet-proof clothing. An engineer calculated that in theory, web silk scaled up to the width of a pencil has the elasticity and recoiling properties to stop a 747 aircraft.

Spider silk was used in pre-industrial times to dress wounds, and its many possible uses in engineering and medicine, including synthesizing it, have been the object of considerable study. But so far it has not been successfully farmed, in part because spiders tend to eat each other when living in groups large enough to spin a harvestable amount of web silk.

Silk is thought to have emerged in spiders' ancestors around 375 million years ago. The first araneid orb webs were spun as recently as 141 million years ago, if araneid orb webs evolved independently of cribellate webs, or as long ago as 247 million years, if orb webs had a single evolutionary origin.

Spider web designs are in general specific down to genus, but can vary in minor ways by species. Individual spiders can adjust the properties of their silk to suit the needs of the moment; some araneids spin thicker draglines as they grow larger, to ensure the line is strong enough to hold them when they fall, and some cobweb weavers can adjust the diameter of wrapping silk to suit the energy level of captured prey. In some cases, younger spiders weave more meticulous constructions than do older spiders; young cross spiders (*Araneus diadematus*) tend to weave more radii into their orb webs than do adults. A recently discovered South American species of what likely will be categorized in the *Cyclosa* genus creates an effigy of itself, presumably as a kind of camouflage.

What this means about a spider's intelligence or possible intentions exactly, no one knows, of course. But when you watch a spider busily paying out silk, deftly working strands in its claws, tying off lines, incorporating unusual "decorations" (a word used by arachnologists), and knowing, somehow, that the overall construction project requires a scaffolding on which to assemble the frame of the web proper, you, or I at least, have to think something more is going on than pure mechanical impulse—"if design govern in a thing so small." ✳

This orbweaver (*Araneus nordmanni*) spun its web between the doorframe and mirror of the car, and remained steady through a half-hour drive from Bangor to Troy.

ORBWEAVERS

Family Araneidae

The orbweaving spiders might be the spiders you're most apt to notice casually because of their beautiful webs and because they're numerous.

Orbweavers come in many sizes and shapes, from 1.5 (six one-hundredths of an inch) to 28 mm (more than an inch) in body length and ranging from large, rather round-shaped abdomens with relatively smaller cephalothorax, to exotic-looking forms with rounded humps as on barn spiders (*Araneus cavaticus*), or protruding, almost spiny humps as on the starbellied orbweaver (*Acanthepeira stellata*).

Orbweavers' webs are the classic spiral webs you often see hanging in a vertical or near-vertical plane in gardens, brush, or the corners of buildings. They are carefully engineered by the spiders in methodical building phases. In general, the spider lays out a framework of silk lines, then builds a scaffolding on which she works to construct the main web, attaching lines at precise angles. When the main web is finished, she takes the scaffolding down. Some orbweavers, such as the black-and-yellow garden spider (*Argiope aurantia*) and the banded garden spider (*Argiope trifasciata*), include a dense squiggle of silk, called a stabilimentum, at the center of the web. Some, like the trashline spider (*Cyclosa*), adorn spokes of the web with bits of vegetation and insect body parts.

Araneus saevus can be distinguished from other angulate, or shoulder-humped, spiders by the light-colored median line at the front of the abdomen.

A large orbweaver in a doorframe in Farmington, Maine.

A lichenmarked orbweaver (*Araneus bicentarius*) found on a road in Waterboro, Maine. Photo courtesy of Frank Allen.

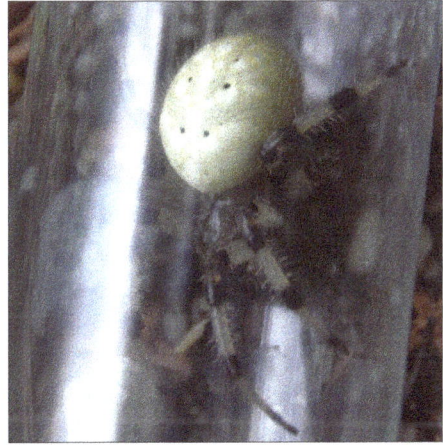

A shamrock orbweaver (*Araneus trifolium*) captured in Steuben, Maine.

The longjawed orbweavers, family Tetragnathidae, also build orb webs, but usually lay them out more horizontally to the ground, normally with fewer spokes radiating from an open center, giving the web an overall more spacious appearance than araneid webs.

Most araneids have poor vision and rely on vibrations of the web silk to tell them whether a meal has been caught. They either sit in the center of the web waiting for bugs to get snared, or retreat to a hiding place, wait for vibrations of the silk, and then run out onto the web and paralyze the prey with a bite. Sometimes they eat right on the spot, but may also wrap the morsel in silk for later.

Most araneids live one or two years. The life cycle for many species involves eggs laid in early fall that may hatch in late fall, with the spiderlings overwintering in the egg sac, or that may hatch in spring or early summer. The

35

spiders mature by early summer, mating and laying the next generation of eggs in a silk egg sac in the fall.

The more than 3,000 species of araneids listed in the *World Spider Catalog* make up 7 percent of all known spider species, and in Maine roughly 40 species have been documented. Jennings and Graham's Milbridge study turned up about 500 individuals in 24 species, the fifth most abundant family in the study.

The word *Araneus* derives from the Latin word araneus, meaning spider.

Larinioides male.

Arabesque orbweaver (*Neoscona arabesca*).

Garden spider webs.

A male araneid.

Starbellied orbweaver (*Acanthepeira stellata*). Photo by James Reben.

Barn spider (*Araneus cavaticus*).

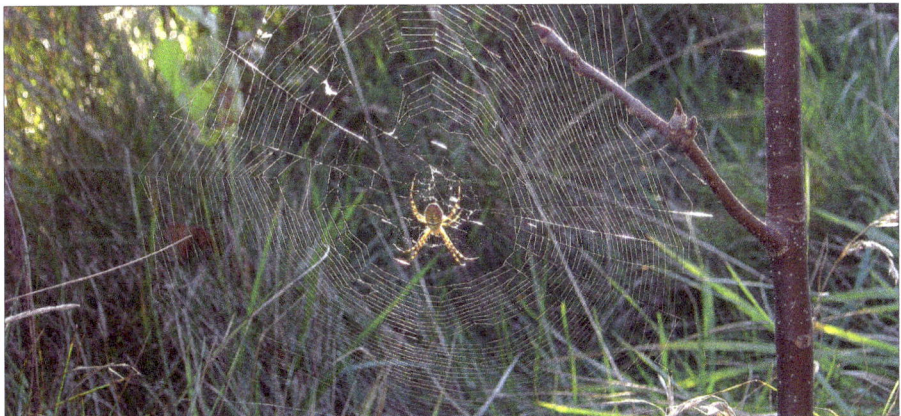

A banded garden spider (*Argiope trifasciata*) in her web.

37

Barn spider (*Araneus cavaticus*)

Barn spiders are among the larger "angulate" spiders, referring to the humps on its back where you might envision shoulders. It's usually gray and hairy, with slightly darker folium, or markings, on its back, and can be difficult to distinguish from *A. nordmanni* and *A. saevus*. The female's web is often very large, up to 10 feet in diameter, and spun in doorframes and corners of buildings, fences, and rocky cliffs. A barn spider was the model for E.B. White's Charlotte A. Cavatica in *Charlotte's Web*.

A barn spider.

The Unity Charlotte in early summer.

The Unity Charlotte

In the middle of July one summer a huge barn spider set up shop in a door frame corner in a shed at the Unity park. An extended family of her species has made its living on that shed summer after summer, meaning generation after generation, for years.

What was amazing was her size. Upwards of three-quarters of an inch in total body length, hairy all over, gray with light mottling on her back, humps on her "shoulders," and banded legs. She belonged to the species *Araneus cavaticus*, the model for E.B. White's character in *Charlotte's Web*. In the book, Charlotte A. Cavatica describes herself as "a sedentary spider," and sure enough, the Unity Charlotte stayed parked in her door-frame orb

August.

web throughout August and September. One day she'd be backed tight into the corner. The next she'd be an inch or two along, still facing out.

The anchoring lines of her web ran all the way out to the other three corners of the door frame, with a

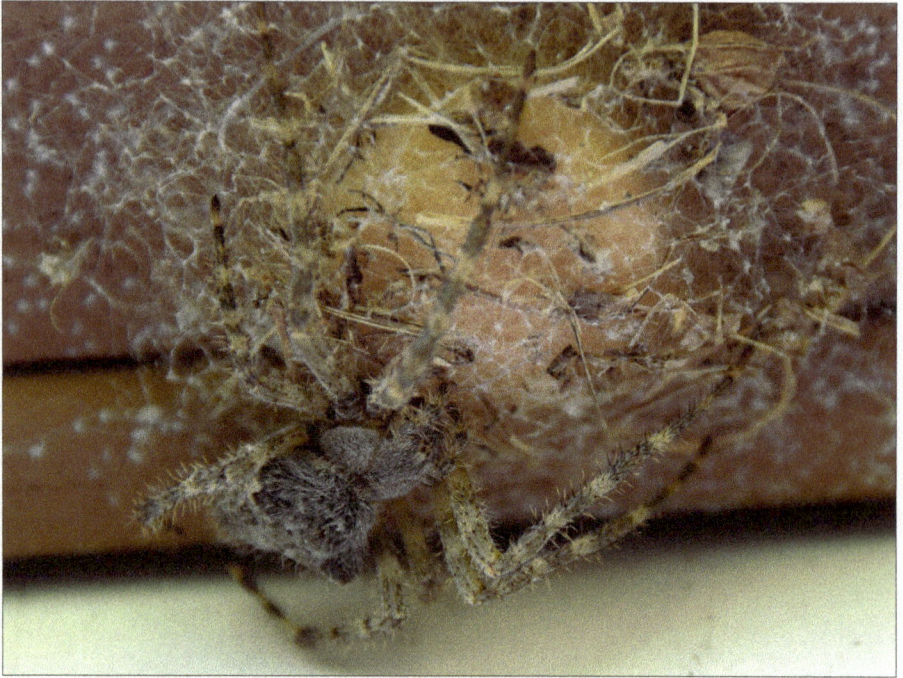

With her egg sac in October.

hefty layer spun somewhat raggedly in between. Her silkwork probably snagged dozens of flies, moths, aphids, and mosquitoes. It was so craftily constructed that you could almost imagine words appearing in the weave. Needless to say, spiders can't write. But at the same time there is almost certainly—in my reading of the natural world, anyway—a formidable intelligence behind engineering that intricate.

Around the end of September she shifted operations to the upper right corner of the door frame and started work on her egg sac. It was a convex tangle of gray, white, and peach colors that grew over a day or two to about 2 inches across. Whether it had 514 eggs in it, as Charlotte's did, I don't know, of course. But one afternoon I noticed her abdomen had shrunk considerably.

When I came back afternoons through October to check on her, she was perched snugly by the sac. Some days she straddled it, with her eight long legs splayed—protectively, I guess—over its whole span. She had stopped tending the orb web, which had become tattered, suggesting she was no longer eating, and she seemed a little more haggard every day.

Some *A. cavaticus* females survive

Spiderlings soon after hatching in June.

winter, in a kind of hibernation prob- ably, and live to early spring. This one was still standing guard over the sac in November. I stopped just about every day to check. Thanksgiving went by, and she was still there. I wasn't always sure she hadn't died there with her feet tacked upside down to the door frame. Around the first of December, despite some cold nights, she was still there. Some spider.

Then one day in the second week of December, she was gone. The egg sac was unmoved on the door frame. I looked down, and sure enough, her dead body was sprawled stiff on the door sill. I carefully collected it and took it home in honor of maternal devotion.

Snow and ice sealed me out of the park for more than four months. When I returned in April, the egg sac, gray- and peach-colored, was still there. I checked it every day in May. By the first week of June, the sac was unchanged. I began to think the eggs had somehow succumbed. Then in mid-June, I stopped to look one more time, and all around the sac and the door frame were dozens of tiny spi- derlings.

Some of them would probably go ballooning soon. Many would get eat- en by predators. But some might stay, judging by the clan that seemed to in- habit this shed summer after summer in a cycle of life indelible. ✳

Cross orbweaver (*Araneus diadematus*)

The cross orbweaver is a large, conspicuous spider found in gardens and brush, and on the sides of buildings. It can vary in color from gray to reddish-orange and gets its name from spots on the upper part of its abdomen that form a cross, though in some individuals this is not obvious. The cross spiders I've seen in central Maine seem to have unusually prominent humped "shoulders" and more elongated abdomens than individuals shown in some guidebooks.

Cross spiders build fresh webs in the morning and spend most of the day there awaiting prey. Adult males are found mainly in late summer, and most females are thought to die by winter, with the young overwintering in the egg sac as either unhatched eggs or as juveniles.

Two cross orbweavers, named Arabella and Anita, traveled to Skylab in the summer of 1973, where their web-building activities were monitored. After some initial trouble in the construction, probably due to the lack of gravity, the spiders built five webs, one of which was fairly normally constructed, while the other four were smaller than normal with very irregular spacing in the radii—"somewhat comparable to webs built after a medium dose of d-amphetamine," according to arachnologists who studied photos of the webs. A spider in space is like a spider on drugs, apparently.

The cross spider was probably introduced from Europe a century or more ago, and its range is mainly the Northeast and the Northwest, including Alaska; it has been found recently in Midwestern states, too. No *A. diadematus* individuals were collected in Jennings and Graham's Milbridge study, but the earlier unpublished version of Jennings and Donahue's checklist of Maine spiders indicates authenticated findings in Maine.

A cross spider (*Araneus diadematus*) hangs in her web in a doorframe in Orrington, Maine. Photo by Joel Crabtree.

Arabella rests on her web in outer space. She was one of two cross spiders sent to Skylab in 1973 for studies on how weightlessness affected web building. Photo courtesy of NASA.

Marbled orbweaver (*Araneus marmoreus*)

The marbled orbweaver comes in a variety of colors, from bright orange or yellow to brownish. It weaves an orb web in a leaf, usually with a tubular retreat in the web's upper corner, in woods and gardens, or on fences or eaves and underneath steps. In overall shape and size it resembles the shamrock orbweaver (*A. trifolium*), and in its less colorful forms the lichenmarked orbweaver (*A. bicentarius*), the barn spider (*A. cavaticus*), *A. nordmanni*, and *A. saevus*. The latter four species are "angulate," meaning they have humps that look like shoulders, whereas *A. marmoreus* has no humps. The marbled orbweaver is also known as the halloween spider, as females are often seen on the ground in October preparing to lay eggs. The eggs overwinter in their sacs; some females may overwinter as subadults.

A marbled orbweaver (*Araneus marmoreus*) under the back step.

A marbled orbweaver (*Araneus marmoreus*) mottled form, living under a plant pot in early August

The same marbled orbweaver in early September.

43

Araneus nordmanni

Sometimes known as Nordmann's orbweaver, *Araneus nordmanni* is a large spider that lives mainly in and around woods and brush. Silk that hits you in the face when walking through woods often belongs to *A. nordmanni*, and it sometimes builds its web under the eaves of buildings. The spider in this photo set up shop underneath our deck railing, and spent much of her time waiting in a retreat in a corner. With its slight shoulder humps and mottled or foliated, dark-brown or black and white abdomen, *A. nordmanni* in size and shape can be difficult to distinguish from the barn spider (*A. cavaticus*), *A. saevus*, and other large "angulate" (having shoulder humps) orbweavers. The eggs hatch in spring or in late fall, with spiderlings overwintering in leaf litter. Jennings and Graham turned up numerous individuals in their Milbridge study.

The Swedish arachnologist Tamerlan Thorell bestowed the species name to honor his colleague, the 19th century Finnish naturalist Alexander von Nordmann.

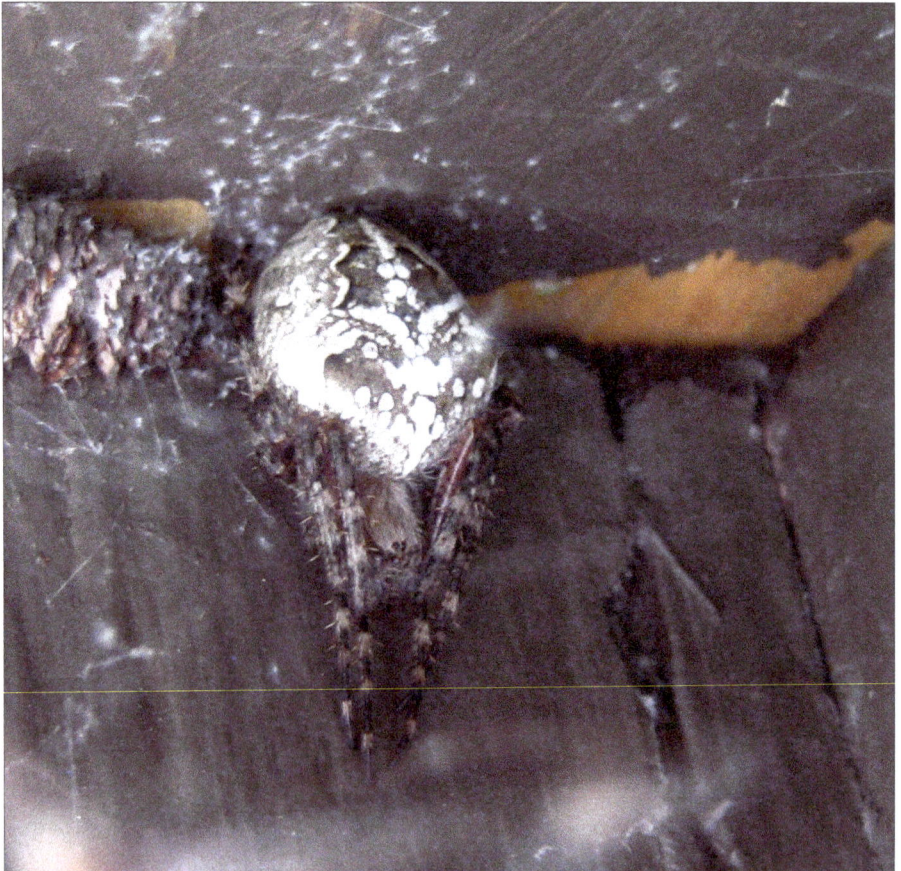

Araneus nordmanni resting near her web under the deck railing.

Six-spotted orbweaver (*Araniella displicata*)

The six-spotted orbweavers often seen around our house and yard have distinctive abdomens, usually red-brown or orange, sometimes lighter colored, with two rows of three conspicuous dark spots along the rear edges. They weave tiny webs in tall grass or brush, or inside the curl of a leaf. I've seen them on the side of the house, in the leaves of a young ash tree, and even inside the house. A study in Manitoba found the six-spotted orbweaver to be a winter-active spider, unlike many orbweavers, meaning it moves around and feeds, to some extent, under the snow.

While this six-spotted orbweaver (*Araniella displicata*) was spending a couple of days in late June in captivity in a vial, she spun her sac and laid her eggs.

The six-spotted orbweaver's egg sac in mid-July, containing probably about 85 eggs.

The six-spotted orbweaver's hatchlings later in July.

Black-and-yellow garden spider (*Argiope aurantia*)

The black-and-yellow garden spider is one of our most conspicuous spiders. The females are fairly large (up to 28 mm (1.1 inches) in body length), and are black with striking yellow marks on their abdomens. They build their large orb webs in sunlit brush and sometimes on buildings, and often weave a dense squiggle of silk, called a stabilimentum, in the center. Many orbweavers are nocturnal, but black-and-yellow garden spiders are diurnal, sitting upside down at the center of their webs during the day. In many spider species adult males are smaller than adult females, and the *A. aurantia* males are a lot smaller (as small as 5 mm, two-tenths of an inch, in body length) and less distinctively marked with yellow; they sometimes build their own webs near or even adjacent to a female's much larger structure.

The genus name *Argiope* is most likely derived from a proper name in Greek mythology, possibly the wife of Orpheus (an alternative name to Eurydice) or more likely the mother of Cadmus, the founder of Thebes, according to Cameron. The Greek Αργιοπη is formed from αργης (argys, "white, gleaming") and -οπη (-opi, "face" or "eye"), thus meaning "with bright face or bright eye."

Above: A black-and-yellow garden spider (*Argiope aurantia*) in her web.

Right: A black-and-yellow garden spider wrapping up her prey.

Banded garden spider (*Argiope trifasciata*)

The banded garden spider sets up shop during the day in the same kind of low brush as the black-and-yellow garden spiders. They are about the same size (females up to 25 mm (1 inch), males as small as 4 mm (.16 inch) body length), often with a slightly more pointed abdomen and less strikingly marked—where the black-and-yellow garden spider has bright yellow splotches or lightning bolt-like markings, the banded garden spider has horizontal black lines with yellow or silver bands between them. The male sometimes lives in the same web with the female.

A banded garden spider (*Argiope trifasciata*).

Trashline orbweaver (*Cyclosa conica*)

Trashline spiders spin orb webs with a relatively large number of spokes and a vertical stabilimentum on which they string the inedible remnants of prey, such as moth wings, and bits of dried leaves. The small spider lives camouflaged at the center of the web, and if disturbed may set the entire web vibrating.

Among trashline spiders, only the females build orb webs, usually in grasses and shrubs, sometimes evergreen trees, and in and on buildings. I've found trashline webs in the bay window of the house, and one particularly beautiful web between the living room sofa and coffee table. Not all webs are "decorated" with debris, but the spider is still so small that it's difficult to spot in the web, which she leaves only rarely, including to affix the egg sac to nearby leaves or twigs. They overwinter in their immature instars.

Cyclosa conica is the species found in New England and eastern Canada, and is identified by a pronounced conical-shaped hump at the back of its abdomen. Its cousin, *C. turbinata*, has an additional two humps near the center of the abdomen. *C. turbinata* is not listed in the Milbridge study or in the earlier unpublished version of Jennings and Donahue's checklist.

The genus name *Cyclosa* comes from the Greek κυκλοω "to move in a circle," referring to the spider's motion while it spins its web. The 19th century German naturalist Anton Menge first described the "Kreisspinne," or circle spider, according to Cameron.

Trashline orbweaver.

Trashline Spiders

In the latter part of summer, unkempt-looking orb webs sometimes appear in conspicuous places around the deck of the house. By unkempt I mean not that the spinning is bad, but that clots of debris and detritus such as moth wings and tiny twigs get hung up in the webwork.

Hardly glancing at them for a long time, I carelessly wrote off these webs as just old and disused. But one September morning I got looking at one under the railing beside the front door, and realized there was a method to the debris madness. It was a trashline web.

The detritus in this web formed a neat, straight line of carefully affixed insect body parts—bits of legs, shells, and torn wings. I turned a magnifying glass on the underside of the railing, thinking the spider might be waiting there for the prey to get tangled up. I couldn't see anybody, so I went back to the fascinating trash line.

After a few minutes I spotted in the tight-knit center of the web a tiny spider, maybe 3 millimeters in body length, with color and shape similar to the insect bits. The eight little legs were folded neatly in, and the abdomen appeared to have a protrusion. This was indeed a trashline spider, *Cyclosa conica*, which is more likely to be seen in Maine than *C. turbinata*, a similar spider but with two little humps on its back.

There is no consensus among arachnologists about what purpose web trash lines serve. A number of orb-weaving spiders decorate their webs with heavy silk lines, sometimes in zigzags, sometimes central spirals, called stabilimenta. *Cyclosa conica* does that, but in some cases takes the decoration (a word the scientists actually use, often seeming unaware of its metaphorical implications) a step further and lines the

A trashline spider in its web.

web with leftovers, sometimes in a straight line like my spider, sometimes in a pattern.

Some arachnologists hypothesize that the trash provides camouflage for the spider. Different studies have found different rates of predation on spiders who use detritus camouflage. One study of a Japanese species of *Cyclosa* found that dummy spiders in trash line webs had substantially fewer wasp bites than dummy spiders without trash lines. On the other hand, a different study on live spiders seemed to show the opposite.

Another hypothesis about the trash lines is that they're meant to attract prey. But again, different studies trying to find out if this is the case have gotten different results. One study found that the trash-lined webs actually had less success attracting food items than undecorated webs.

One uncertainty involves what predators actually see when they look at a trashline web. I couldn't see the spider until I got the magnifying glass out, but my vision is quite a bit different from a wasp's or a bird's. Many insects can see wavelengths of light that humans can't, and spider silks reflect ultraviolet light in varying intensities. Humans can't see ultraviolet light, so we don't know exactly what the web looks like to a wasp.

What it looks like to me, on the other hand, is kind of fascinating. The

trash in our spider's web was arranged in a very straight, evenly spaced line. An Asian species, *C. confusa*, arranges the trash to resemble its own size and shape, presumably as a decoy. And a few years ago, some researchers in the Peruvian Amazon stumbled across a spider (which they believe is probably a new species of *Cyclosa*) that constructs what amounts to a replica of itself—down to the legs, cephalothorax, and abdomen—and hides underneath the trash effigy.

What's happening in a spider's mind when it carefully spins a beautiful, symmetrical orb web, and then puts heavier threads of silk or bits and pieces of insect parts into it, like designs in a carpet? No scientist, or metaphor, can say.

One night later that September, another web appeared with anchoring lines up to about 3 feet between the deck railing and the bay window of the house. At the center was what looked like an araneid, with two body parts and distinct legs, way too large to be *Cyclosa*. I couldn't see it clearly in the dark.

When I got up the next morning, the web was still there. But what had looked in the dark like a large spider turned out to be a bunch of detritus in the shape of a spider, with two oblong body sections, jointed legs.

I don't know. I can only describe the form I saw. But I can't stop pointing to the beauty. ✳

Bridge orbweaver (*Larinioides sclopetarius*)

The bridge orbweaver, also known as the gray cross spider, spins its webs on bridges, fences, and the sides of buildings. I frequently see them in my walks near Unity Pond. Its cousin the furrow orbweaver (*L. cornutus*) also tends to live near lake shores. Both species have particularly rich markings, or folia, on their dark abdomens, and bridge spiders sometimes build nearby each other in high densities. *Larinioides sclopetarius* is thought to have been introduced from Europe.

Larinioides patagiatus, which tends to be a more reddish color, also turned up in Jennings and Graham's Milbridge study. In November 2008, one was flown to the International Space Station along with a labyrinth orbweaver (*Metepeira labyrinthea*), where the astronauts watched them spin webs in near-zero gravity. Since araneids' normal construction process involves dropping down from threads—an operation impossible without gravity—the webs were a random mess at first. But remarkably, after a few days and a lot of flailing of legs, the spiders figured out how to fashion awkward-looking, but stable spiral webs.

Two species of *Metepeira* are documented in Maine, according to the earlier unpublished version of Jennings and Donahue's checklist, but not *M. labyrinthea*.

Cameron thinks the genus name *Larinioides* may be named with the ancient Italian town Larinum (mentioned by Cicero) in mind, and combined with the Greek suffix -oides, meaning "similar."

Larinioides patagiatus in China, Maine. Photo by James Reben.

A furrow orbweaver (*Larinioides cornutus*). Photo by James Reben.

A bridge orbweaver (*Larinioides sclopetarius*).

Bolas spider (*Mastophora*)

The fascinating bolas spider, of the genus *Mastophora*, lives in orchards and rural yards, often near corn fields. Its hunting method is to create a ball of sticky silk attached to the end of a thread. Holding the thread with a front claw, the spider waits for a moth to approach and, timing to just the right moment, winds up and throws the ball at the moth, entangles it in a loop, and reels it in.

The spider's ball swung on a line is similar to the throwing weapon called a bolas used by South American gauchos, hence the spider's common name.

I've never seen a bolas spider, and the Milbridge study did not find one. But Bradley says it is found in all states except the Northwest, and a BugGuide photo accessed online in 2018 shows a bolas spider identified as *Mastophora bisaccata* found in Otisfield, in Oxford County.

Arabesque orbweaver (*Neoscona arabesca*)

The arabesque orbweaver is a spider I see commonly in my walks through tall grass and brush. They are usually more red than brown, sometimes even appearing orange, and can have dark or light markings on their backs. They are diligent web-menders, in my observations anyway, and are active mostly at night but also during the day, where they're often in a retreat nearby the web. When disturbed in the web they scamper to the retreat. The arabesque orbweaver was one of the 10 most numerous species collected overall in Jennings and Graham's Milbridge study.

An arabesque orbweaver (*Neoscona arabesca*).

A meshweaver, family Dictynidae.

MESHWEAVERS
Family Dictynidae

The meshweavers are mostly very small spiders (around 4 mm (.16 inch) in body length, more and less) that resemble cobweb weavers (family Theridiidae) to some extent. They live under leaf litter and in vegetation, where some of them build small meshlike webs in the tips of dead grass or other brush; some others build sheet-like webs on buildings, fences, and trees. Male and female dictynids are sometimes found co-habiting the web after mating. The females usually produce more than one egg sac. Many dictynid species overwinter in leaf litter as subadults.

The dictynids' silk is meshlike because, like many species of hackledmesh weavers (family Amaurobiidae), most species of meshweavers are cribellate spiders—meaning they have a platelike organ called a cribellum that spins out the silk, which is in turn carded or combed by a series of curved bristles, called a calamistrum, on each of their fourth, or hind legs, giving the silk a somewhat ragged appearance. (Most spiders are ecribellate; that is, most do not have a cribellum.)

The *World Spider Catalog* in 2020 listed 470 species worldwide in the Dictynidae family. The earlier unpublished version of Jennings and Donahue's checklist of Maine spiders indicated numerous identifications of *Dictyna*, *Emblyna*, and *Lathys* genus spiders; but dictynids were among the least abundant families collected in Jennings and Graham's Milbridge study. The Milbridge study lists *Cicurina* as a dictynid, and formerly an agelenid, and it was recently reclassified again from Dictynidae to family Hahniidae.

The genus name *Dictyna* is from an epithet of the goddess Artemis, Δικτυννα (Diktinna), derived from the word for nets used in fishing or hunting.

This comb-tailed spider (*Cicurina robusta*) was living under a tarp over a wood pile in Fairfield, Maine. Photo by James Reben.

COMB-TAILED SPIDERS

Family Hahniidae

The comb-tailed spiders superficially resemble grass spiders (family Ageleni-dae) and meshweavers (family Dictynidae). They are mostly small spiders, often around 2 mm (about .1 inch) in total body length, though some in the sub-family Cryphoecine may be as large as 7.8 mm (more than ¼ inch). They get their common name from the unusual arrangement of six spinnerets in a line on the abdomen of some genera.

Neoantistea genus hahniids spin inconspicuous sheet webs just a few inches wide in small depressions in the ground or moss, and tend to stay underneath the web, which rarely may include a retreat. Some species of comb-tailed spiders are "vagrant" or wandering spiders. *Cicurina* species live under leaf litter and spin a small sheetlike web; some of these are cave-dwellers reported to have just six eyes, and in some cases none.

Hahniids make up one of the spider families that have undergone many tax-onomic changes over the years. Jennings and Graham collected five hahniid spe-cies in their Milbridge study, plus three species of *Cicurina* (formerly Dictynidae) making it the sixth most abundant family collected. The *World Spider Catalog* in 2020 indicates more than 350 species worldwide.

C.L. Koch named the *Hahnia* genus after the German naturalist Carl Wil-helm Hahn, who died in 1836 while he was at work on his magnum opus, *Die Arachniden*. Hahn's "Monographie der Spinnen" was reputedly the first mono-graph on spiders written in German. The family name was coined in 1878.

Spider Bites

Before the 1950s, few people in the continental United States were too concerned about, or had even heard of, brown recluse spiders. There were reports of spiders in Missouri inflicting bites that resulted in fairly nasty skin lesions, so in the mid-1950s some researchers investigated. They noted "a striking similarity" between the symptoms of the bites in Missouri and the "cutaneous arachnoidism" induced by bites from the Chilean recluse spider (*Loxosceles laeta*) studied in the 1930s in South America. Eventually the researchers concluded that the probable culprit in Missouri was *L. laeta*'s cousin, *Loxosceles reclusa*, the brown recluse, whose range is the mid-southern United States. The researchers' 1957 report in *Science* makes no mention of deaths resulting from recluse bites.

However, after the news media got hold of the story, numerous reports of brown recluse bites began to surface. After a while, the fact that brown recluse spider bites can cause necrotic lesions spread from news reports into medical literature and doctors' offices. By the 1990s physicians were often diagnosing necrotic lesions as brown recluse bites even when no spider had been seen, which was usually. At some point it was recognized that "systemic loxoscelism"—as the severest result of a brown recluse bite is known technically—could in rare instances cause death. Arachnologists and entomologists have had an uphill battle disabusing people of deadly spider bite fallacies ever since.

The most important thing to understand about spider bites is this: the vast majority of spiders do not bite human beings. Most spiders bite to subdue prey, not to deter predators. They deliver venom from glands connected to tiny fangs located on the tips of their jaws, or chelicerae, and those mouthparts in most spiders are not large or strong enough to break human skin. Of the roughly 48,000 known spider species, only about 200 of them can inflict a medically significant bite to

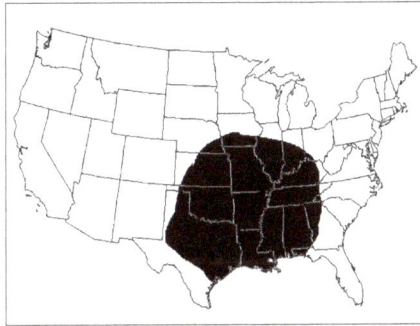

The rough range of brown recluse spiders in the U.S.

humans; only four spider genera can inflict a bite that can result in death.

In North America, two spiders that can deliver medically significant bites are the widow spiders (of the cobweb weavers, family Theridiidae) and the brown recluse spiders (of the six-eyed spiders, family Sicariidae). Individual widow and recluse spiders do turn up in Maine, but only rarely; neither spider's established range reaches as far north as Maine.

Daniel Jennings and Ivan McDaniel in the late 1980s investigated the discovery in Bangor of a female western black widow spider (*Latrodectus hesperus*), which they determined had stowed away in the belongings of a family that had recently driven from Arizona to Maine. In 1981 they also investigated the discovery of a male and a female brown recluse (*Loxosceles reclusa*) and concluded that pair, as well, had been brought accidentally to Maine from Oklahoma. They reported it is not impossible for brown recluse spiders to set up a breeding colony in Maine under the right conditions. But researchers studying cold tolerance of recluse spiders in Illinois have concluded it is unlikely those spiders can become established north of their documented range, whose northernmost extent is southern Illinois and southern Iowa.

Maine winters are just too cold for widow or recluse spiders to have much chance of getting established.

University of Maine Cooperative Extension entomologist Don Barry told me in 2015 that "we've captured a total of three specimens [of brown recluse spiders] and each of these was traced to out-of-state travel; they are not in New England."

Only one black widow bite has ever been reported in Maine, and even in that case the spider is believed to have been misidentified.

Venom and its effects

The venom of widow spiders (genus *Latrodectus*) contains a neurotoxin, which acts on nerve tissue and is designed to paralyze prey. When a widow spider bites a human, symptoms of "latrodectism," including abdominal and facial muscle pain, nausea, or tremors, may begin in a half-hour to two hours. In the vast majority of cases, the symptoms subside within a day or so. In rare cases, muscles in the chest and diaphragm can be affected causing respiration problems, which can lead to heart attack and death. Widow spider bites lead to death in less than 1 percent of the cases in which a human is bitten.

The venom of brown recluse spiders contains a cytotoxin, which damages cell tissue. A human is unlikely to even notice a bite from a recluse spider when it happens. Within a day or two as enzymes destroy flesh around the wound, a lesion may arise that can go from irritating to painful over a few days. Arachnologists refer to this as "cutaneous loxoscelism." Most brown recluse bites are either never noticed or subside within a few days. In unusual cases, the lesions can grow quite large, last months, and require medical care. In rare cases, more severe reactions develop, including systemic problems such as damage to red blood cells, disruption to blood clotting, and renal failure, which in very rare cases can lead to death.

Accurate estimates of how many people are actually bitten each year by widow or recluse spiders are nearly impossible to come by, largely because in many cases no spider is seen. A study by a medical doctor of animal-related fatalities in the U.S. from 1991 to 2001 found 66 people died from venomous spider bites in those 10 years, most of them in the South. Arachnologists are more or less unified in asserting that doctors often misdiagnose as spider bites lesions and infections that were actually caused by allergic reactions to bites by other arthropods or to skin irritants.

Incidents of recluse spiders biting humans are not common, even in places where the spiders are abundant. One researcher counted more than 200 *Loxosceles* webs in a Southern house where no one had ever been bitten.

A few spiders commonly found in Maine do have the capacity to make you remember the encounter, even though their bites are not medically significant. The severity of the experience depends partly on a person's sensitivity to the toxin. Some wolf spiders, jumping spiders, grass spiders, and sac spiders are said to be capable of making an impression on you. But again, they get out of your way first and bite only as a last resort, and effects depend on allergic sensitivities.

In the continental U.S., hobo spiders (the grass spider *Eratigena agrestis*, formerly *Tegenaria agrestis*; family Agelenidae), which live mainly in the Pacific Northwest, have long been rumored to inflict painful bites, but researchers have found little evidence this is true. The spiders most dangerous to humans live in Australia and South America. The male funnel-web spider (*Atrax robustus*) in Australia might have the venom most deadly to humans, though no deaths from its bite have been reported since 1981, around the time antivenom therapies became very effective. ✳

A linyphiid in her web.

SHEETWEB WEAVERS
Family Linyphiidae

The sheetweb weavers, as their name suggests, build sheetlike webs, underneath which members of larger species can be seen hanging upside down. The webs, normally built in trees or brush, consist of one or more roughly horizontal platforms, either sheet, bowl, or dome shaped, over which is woven an irregular tangle of silk. When flying insects are knocked down by the threads above, the spider attacks the bug from underneath, cutting the web, pulling the bug through, paralyzing, and wrapping it. Many linyphiids afterward make repairs to the cuts in the web.

The Linyphiidae are divided into several subfamilies, the two principal ones in Maine being Linyphiinae and Erigoninae (dwarf spiders). The subfamily Linyphiinae of sheetweb weavers comprises small to medium-sized spiders that in general live in vegetation above ground. The Erigoninae, or dwarf spiders, generally live on the ground and are some of the smallest spiders in the world; adults of some species measure less than 1 mm (.04 inch) in body length.

Many sheetweb weavers overwinter either as juveniles or adults, and some have been found active under snow. Research indicates younger linyphiids have a rougher time surviving the cold, but this is not related to size; a study in central Canada showed dwarf spiders, along with some wolf spiders, were most abundant in winter months.

Sheetweb weavers make up the second most numerous family of spiders in the world, with more than 4,600 species listed by the *World Spider Catalog* in 2019, second only to the jumping spiders (family Salticidae). In Maine, sheetweb weavers were the second most numerous family collected in Jennings and Graham's Milbridge study, behind the wolf spiders (family Lycosidae). Jennings and Graham collected 54 species of dwarf spiders, among which *Grammonota angusta* was the tenth most frequently collected species overall in the Milbridge study and one of the more numerous Erigoninae species reported in the earlier unpublished version of Jennings and Donahue's checklist of Maine spiders.

In Great Britain, Australia, and parts of Europe, sheetweb weavers are also known as money spiders, a name apparently adapted from superstitions about certain spiders being good luck when found crawling near or on you.

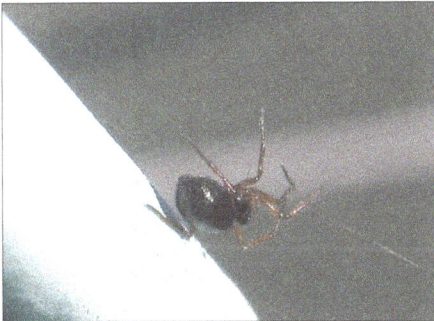

A dwarf sheetweb weaver of the subfamily Erigoninae.

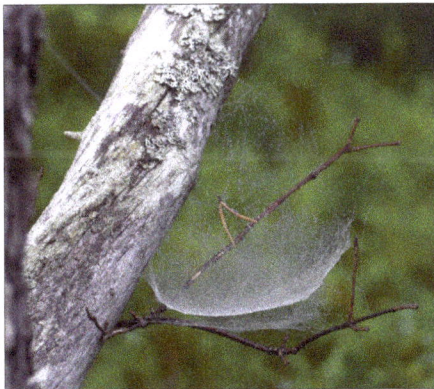

The web of a bowl-and-doily spider in Steuben, Maine.

A bowl-and-doily spider (*Frontinella communis*).

European hammock spider (*Linyphia triangularis*)

The European hammock spider, a medium-sized sheetweb weaver, is one of the more extensively studied spiders in Maine because it's an invasive species that arrived here just in recent decades. As its common name implies, it is a Palearctic, or native Eurasian species whose range extends from Europe to China; it is abundant in Great Britain, and seems to have been introduced from there to the Maine coast, though how is not known. It was first found and identified in Maine in 1991 by Frank Graham, and subsequent research by Graham and Jennings indicated unidentified individuals were collected in the 1980s, with the earliest found in Brooksville in 1983.

Linyphia triangularis seems to have had a more or less immediate impact on the spider community in Acadia National Park, if not elsewhere in Maine. Studies in the 2000s showed that in areas where *L. triangularis* was living in high densities, other sheetweb weavers, such as the native bowl-and-doily spiders (*Frontinella communis*), filmy dome spiders (*Neriene radiata*), and other hammock spiders (*Pityohyphantes* genus), were declining.

At the same time, researchers working in Winter Harbor in 2002 found the kleptoparasite spider *Neospintharus trigonum* (then known as *Argyrodes trigonum*) eating a *L. triangularis* female in her own web, and they found *N. trigonum* indi-

A European hammock spider (*Linyphia triangularis*).

viduals in nearby *L. triangularis* webs, as well. (A kleptoparasite spider steals prey from other spiders' webs.) Jennings had also found a juvenile *Neospintharus* in a *L. triangularis* web in Pittston (Kennebec County) in 1999, suggesting the invasive spider's Maine range was affecting spider ecology beyond the Down East coast.

The mating rituals of *L. triangularis* are unusual among spiders generally. In most spider species, the male's approach to the female is a delicate process, for a number of reasons, one of which is that in some situations female spiders may attack or even eat a mate. But females of *L. triangularis* never threaten the males, who will invade the female's web and even eat her food. The courtship ritual includes the male destroying the female's web over the course of just a few minutes. Arachnologists believe the destruction of the web erases pheromones in the silk that might attract other males to her. The female's lack of response is thought to be her signal of receptiveness to the male.

Cameron explains the name *Linyphia* is derived from the Greek word λινον (linon) meaning "anything made of flax, line, thread, net," together with the feminine ending -ia, giving P.A. Latreille his invention *Linyphia*, "thread-weaver." Jennings and Graham informally nicknamed *L. triangularis* "Linytri" in their notebooks.

Filmy dome spider (*Neriene radiata*)

The filmy dome spider gets its name from its dome-shaped web, typically 4 or 5 inches in diameter, which is often seen in brush, low trees and sometimes among rocks. They are a medium-sized to small spider, around 4 or 5 mm (around one-tenth of an inch) in body length, often with splashes of light yellow on the abdomen, similar to the European hammock spider (*Linyphia triangularis*). Adults and older juveniles overwinter in leaf litter and wood. In spring, male and female filmy dome spiders have been found co-habiting webs.

The genus name *Neriene* is the name in Latin mythology of Mars's wife. It was a synonym for *Linyphia* from the 19th century, according to Cameron.

A filmy dome spider (*Neriene radiata*).

Hammock spider (*Pityohyphantes costatus*)

The hammock spider, one of the larger sheetweb weavers, builds its hammock-shaped web in shrubs and low in trees and waits in the corner of the web or a silk retreat for prey to get tangled up. Jennings and Graham found quite a few individuals on the ground. It is a bit larger than other sheetweb weavers, in the range of 6 mm (around .23 inch) in body length, often with darker folia on a lighter-colored abdomen. Young and adult hammock spiders overwinter under rocks and bark, often entering diapause, the arachnid version of hibernation, or sometimes remaining active.

The genus name *Pityohyphantes* is from the Greek πιτνος ("pine tree") and υφαινω ("weave"), and therefore "pine weaver," according to Cameron.

A hammock spider (*Pityohyphantes costatus*).

Uncivilized Behavior

For an amateur naturalist, I've gotten pretty good at herding small creatures neatly into glass vials to keep and watch. Not wanting to harm them, I always let them go after a day or two.

One morning I spotted a hammock spider, a species of sheetweb weaver, hanging upside down underneath her sheetweb beneath a fence at the Unity park. She was waiting for vibrations in the silk to tell her a bug had been knocked onto the web by the silk strung up over it. Her attack routine would be to open a hole in the sheetweb and pull the bug down through, paralyze it with a bite, and then, at some point, eat it. Afterward she might go back and repair the hole.

I got out my little glass vial, and after a few seconds of spider-herding, sealed her in with the cork stopper. Through my pocket magnifying glass I saw the markings of, most likely, *Pityohyphantes*. Close enough for jazz, like we used to say of guitar-tuning in my rock and roll band long ago. I put the vial and the spider in my pocket and drove home.

In the driveway I was about to shut the car door when something moved on the hood. I leaned over to look. Its big front eyes indicated it was a jumping spider. I only had the one vial, which already contained the hammock spider. Maybe I could herd the jumper in before the sheetweb weaver ran out.

I fished the vial out of my pocket. As luck would have it—for me, at least—the sheetweb weaver was busy spinning some fine threads for what might be a retreat near the glass bottom. So I uncorked the vial, aimed carefully, and set it over the jumper, flush to the hood. Now the

The jumping spider at the top of this photo battled, subdued, and eventually consumed the sheetweb weaver seen paralyzed here at the bottom of their captivity vial.

trick was to get the cork back on without jamming the jumper's legs, or worse, letting him escape.

More good luck. He ran toward the inside of the vial. So the cork slipped neatly on, spider's legs in no danger. I congratulated myself on my civilized respect for tiny life.

Inside the vial, though, was another world of monsters, dreams, and discord.

The hammock spider immediately ran at the jumping spider. They boxed for a second then dashed for opposite ends of the vial. In the next little while, the jumping spider explored the cork end of the vial while the hammock spider worked silk in the glass end. From time to time the hammock spider appeared to forget the situation and wandered toward the jumper. She would suddenly halt, seem to stare for a moment like the proverbial spider in the headlights, then scamper back to the glass end.

When I looked through the magnifying lens, the jumper appeared to be a male *Eris militaris*, aka bronze jumper, common in these parts. (Although this is some very loose jazz, here—jumping spiders are notoriously difficult to ID to species.) Anyway, the standoff in the vial continued. This probably was not going to end well for one of the spiders. Would the jumping spider eat the sheetweb weaver, or the other way around? Or neither?

My attention wandered to a Doors album that had been seething my savage breast recently. Beautiful music,

but ominous and dark. A few songs later, Bonnie asked what my new spiders were doing (hoping I had put the tiny monsters outside, I'm sure). As I started to describe their so-far peaceful co-existence, I checked the vial and saw they were face to face in the middle.

There were feints, lunges, backings off. Then suddenly they were grappling. Long jointed legs furiously pumping.

The struggle went on for maybe 15 or 20 seconds. Then the wrestling stopped. They seemed to have jammed their faces together. For several minutes it was not clear that either one had prevailed. The jumping spider adjusted its legs as if to get a better grip. The hammock spider seemed to be trying futilely to work the jumping spider. Within a couple of minutes, the hammock spider's longer, spindlier legs were markedly less motile. As you would expect of paralyzing poison, soon they were not moving at all. The jumper used a few threads of silk to tie off any remaining resistance, then retreated to his end of the vial.

Around lunchtime, Bonnie asked if anything was left of the hammock spider. With the Doors jazzing in the background, I checked, and the jumping spider was positioned face-first at the hammock spider's abdomen. He'd sunk his chelicerae in, and was now injecting digestive juices and sucking out the meal. I think behind the veil the hammock spider was probably still alive at that point.

We had a nice chicken salad for lunch. ✳

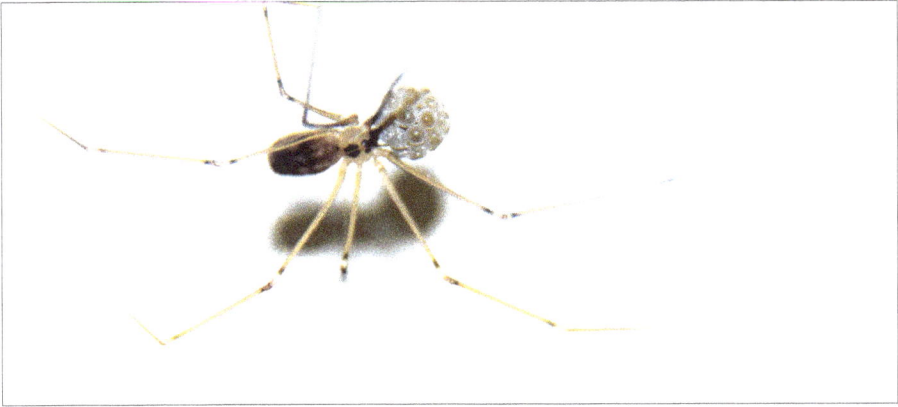

A mother cellar spider (*Pholcus*) holding her egg sac in Steuben, Maine.

CELLAR SPIDERS
Family Pholcidae

The two species of cellar spider found in Maine, *Pholcus manueli* and *Pholcus phalangioides*, are identifiable in part by their unusually long, thin legs. Because of these long legs, the longbodied cellar spider (*P. phalangioides*) is sometimes called the daddylonglegs spider. But it's a spider, not what we conventionally call a daddy long-legs, which is actually a harvestman, of the Opiliones order. (Spiders are of the Araneae order.) You can distinguish a daddy long-legs from a cellar spider by the shapes of their bodies: Daddy long-legs appear to have just one round body part on long stilts, whereas cellar spiders have the two body parts—cephalothorax and abdomen.

Cellar spiders build varying designs of webs, from domed sheets with a tangle of silk over them, to cobwebs with no sheet, to, in some species, just a few strands of silk close to the ground. They generally hang upside down in the web, often located in dark corners and ceilings, and wait for prey. When they feel threatened, they flex their legs rapidly and set themselves gyrating so quickly in the web that they look like a blur. Some araneids, such as the black-and-yellow garden spider (*Argiope aurantia*), also vibrate their webs when threatened.

Some cellar spiders capture other spiders, sometimes much larger than themselves, by creating vibrations in the other spider's web that seem like vibrations from a captured insect. When the web owner rushes out, the cellar spider, using its long legs, draws silk from its spinnerets and throws it until the victim is entangled and can be safely approached and bitten.

Female cellar spiders wrap their eggs in a few strands of silk and carry them around in their chelicerae, or mouth parts, until the eggs hatch. In some species, males remain with the female until the eggs hatch, and in many species, males and females live together peacefully in adjacent web networks. Males sometimes turn their meals over to the females, an unusual practice among spiders, possibly to ensure she stays around the web.

Cellar spiders have adapted to human habitations and overwinter, through their relatively long lives of two or more years, in cellars and basements.

Pholcus species are thought to be native to Eurasia and to have emigrated with humans to many parts of the world, including Alaska and northern Canada. Just one species of cellar spider (*P. manueli*) was identified in the Milbridge study, but Jennings and Graham believed *P. phalangioides* to be present as well. The shortbodied cellar spider (*Spermophora senoculata*) has been identified twice in Maine, once in Penobscot County and once in my basement in Troy; it is a tiny, six-eyed species, introduced to North America.

The *World Spider Catalog* in 2019 listed more than 1,700 species of cellar spider worldwide, with dozens of species in the *Pholcus* genus.

Cameron says the name *Pholcus* comes from the ancient Greek word φολκος, (pholkos) which occurs only in Homer's *Iliad* and was thought to mean "bandy-legged" or in ancient times "squinting" or "squint-eyed." The 19th century French naturalist Charles Walckenaer, who was responsible for many of the original scientific names of spiders, probably "meant to refer to the eye arrangement of *Pholcus*, namely six eyes arranged in triangular groups of three on each side of the cephalothorax, plus two anterior median eyes," according to Cameron.

A shortbodied cellar spider (*Spermophora senoculata*).

An Eastern harvestman, or daddy long-legs.

Daddy Long-Legs

At our house, daddy long-legs crawl all over the outside of everywhere during the fall. Their official common name is harvestmen. Spiders and harvestmen are both arachnids (in the class Arachnida), but spiders are in the order Araneae, and harvestmen are in the order Opiliones. (Ticks and mites are arachnids, too, but in the order Acarina.) Harvestmen are not to be confused with the longbodied cellar spider (*Pholcus phalangioides*), which is sometimes also called the daddylonglegs spider because of its long, thin legs.

No one minds the harvestmen at our house, the way some of us (who are not me) mind spiders. The main thing, I think, is that while spiders look like they'd tear your face off and gnash it down if they were only a little bigger, daddy long-legs don't look the least bit fierce. They amble around on these huge stilts acting like they're more curious than anything else. I was told when very young—and I imagine most everybody else learned the same folklore—that daddy long-legs don't bite, which I'm pretty sure made me feel well-disposed toward them.

It turns out this folklore is true—they don't bite humans. Daddy long-legs have neither fangs nor venom. They're mainly scavengers, prowling the side of the house and vegetation looking for small insects, mites, or newly dead arthropods, even spiders, to eat, and some of them nibble decaying plants and fungi or even bird droppings.

They appear to have just one round body part, but if you look closely there are two, like spiders; but unlike spiders, the joint between the sections is so fat that harvestmen look like they're all head, and the vast majority have just two eyes. Their long, thready legs have olfactory and breathing organs. They also have stink glands under the first and second pairs of legs, and some of them apparently use their pedipalps, the handlike appendages near their mouths, to mix the acrid-smelling secretion with saliva and throw it at predators.

The second pair of legs is the longest and used like antennae to feel out the ground for things to eat. Daddy long-legs can lose one of the first, third, or fourth sets of legs and hobble on, even though lost legs don't regenerate, but damage to one of the second pair is usually fatal. Interestingly, while their mating procedure starts off as basically a surprise attack by the male, once the brief copulatory embrace is under way (male opilionids are the only arachnid with a penis), the couple gently stroke each other with those long legs. Sometimes on cold nights large groups of them gather in a protected place such as the side of a building and interlace their legs in "a nightmarish hairball," as one field guide puts it. No one knows exactly why they do this. Maybe for warmth, but no one knows for sure.

In Maine we most commonly see the Eastern harvestmen (*Leiobunum vittatum*) and the brown harvestmen (*Phalangium opilio*). They scoot around the wood pile, along the deck railing and side of the house, and over plants with a kind of leisurely arachnoid grace. Most of them do not live through winter. They push their eggs into soil, moss, or rotten wood, and the next generation ambles out the following summer to relieve us of some of our bugs and help give the backyard the familiar shape of fall. ✳

A longjawed orbweaver.

LONGJAWED ORBWEAVERS
Family Tetragnathidae

The longjawed orbweavers are distinguished in most species by their long, thin bodies and legs, and long, heavy-looking chelicerae (mouth parts) with often prominent fangs. Because they build orb webs, they used to be classified with orbweavers (araneids), but anatomical differences, most of them inconspicuous, prompted the arachnologists to place them in their own family.

Longjawed orbweavers' webs are often seen near and even over brooks and small ponds, and many of these spiders can run on the water. Other species live in marshes, fields, and woodland vegetation, and the cave orbweaver (*Meta ovalis*) lives in dark places such as caves and crevices.

Longjawed orbweavers' snares differ in two frequently seen ways from the orb webs of araneids. First, while most orbweavers' webs are spun more or less vertically to the ground, most longjawed orbweavers' webs are spun at oblique angles or even horizontally to the ground. Second, longjawed orbweavers' webs often have a looser appearance because they generally are empty at the center, whereas orbweavers' centers have a distinct hub (and sometimes more em-

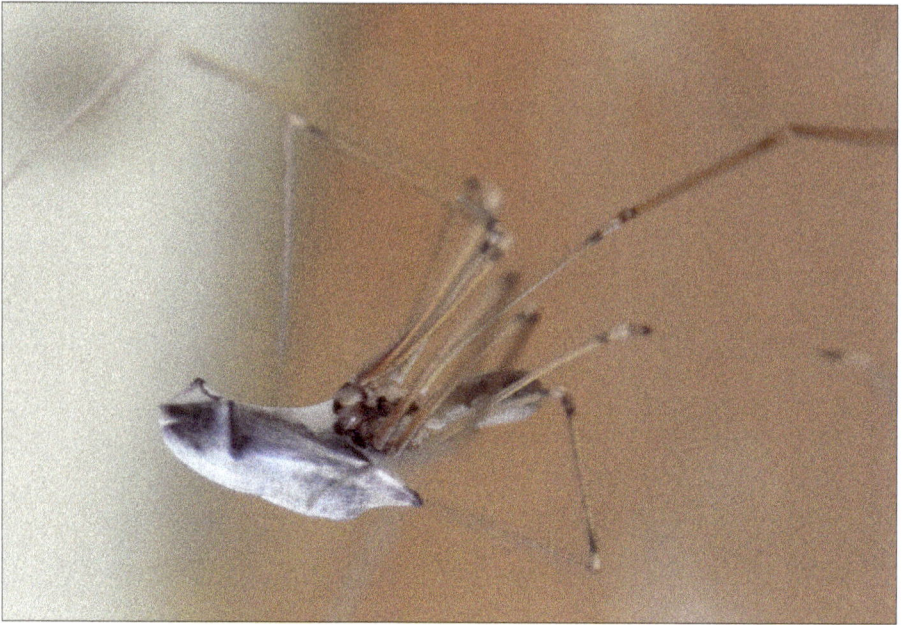

A longjawed orbweaver with its catch.

bellishments); and longjawed orbweavers' webs oftentimes have fewer radial threads than do orbweavers'. One study found that *Tetragnatha* webs tended to have about 18 radial threads, while for comparison, webs of the small araneid *Mangora* tended to have 50 to 60 radial threads. Interestingly, studies have revealed that in comparison to araneids, tetragnathids use different legs in finely different processes when constructing their webs, including in some cases spinning a hub at the center in the early, scaffolding stages and then biting it out for the finished orb.

Many species of tetragnathid are winter-active on or under snow with, in some cases, their reproduction period in winter. Some even build webs and catch prey (such as springtails) in temperatures below freezing (32 degrees Fahrenheit).

Tetragnathidae were the 13th-most abundant family collected (out of 19 categories) in Jennings and Graham's Milbridge study, but worldwide it is one of the most abundant families of spiders, with the *World Spider Catalog* in 2019 listing just more than 1,000 species worldwide.

Cameron explains that the use of the Greek word τετραγναθοσ, meaning four-jawed—τετρα (tetra, "four"); γναθοσ (gnathos, "jaw")—to refer to some kind of spider in South Asia goes back to at least the first century B.C. The word continued to turn up with respect to spiders over the centuries, and finally the 18th century French naturalist Pierre André Latreille used it as the basis for the genus name *Tetragnatha*.

Cave orbweaver (*Meta ovalis*)

The cave orbweaver makes its web in dark places, such as cave entrances, deep rock crevices, culverts, and other well-shaded spots. The male pictured here was moving cautiously around the debris by the firewood pile next to the wall of the Shed; a guess is that a female may have had a web underneath the Shed floor. The web has an open hub, like those of most tetragnathids, and may be 25-40 cm (10-16 inches) in diameter. The female suspends her egg sac from a thread near the web and guards it until the spiderlings hatch. These spiders overwinter as subadults and mature the next spring and summer.

Cameron says the 19th century naturalist Carl Ludwig Koch took this genus name from Greek mythology: Meta (Μετα) was the first of two wives of Aegeus, the mythic founder of Athens, who did not bear him any children.

A cave orbweaver (*Meta ovalis*).

Thick-jawed orbweaver (*Pachygnatha autumnalis*)

The thick-jawed orbweavers generally have more rounded bodies than most tetragnathids, and the males have especially large chelicerae (mouth parts) even for this family. They spin snare webs as juveniles, but after they mature make their livings as wandering hunters, an exception to the tetragnathids' orbweaving lifestyles. They are winter-active spiders.

Cameron says the genus name *Pachygnatha* is formed from the Greek words παχυς (pachos, "thick") and γναθος (gnathos, "jaw") to mean thick-jawed, and, moreover, to make a rhyme with *Tetragnatha*.

A thick-jawed orbweaver (*Pachygnatha autumnalis*).

Longjawed orbweavers (*Tetragnatha*)

Among the longjawed orbweavers, species in the *Tetragnatha* genus are commonly seen in Maine, but are difficult to distinguish from each other without close anatomical inspection. Seven different species were collected in Jennings and Graham's Milbridge study, and the early version of Jennings and Donahue's checklist of Maine spiders indicated 11 species identified in Maine. They build horizontal webs, often in bushes near water, on the surface of which they can run nimbly. Members of *T. versicolor*, which resemble the spider pictured here, often rest on twigs with their long legs stretched out in front of them, making them difficult for predators to spot.

A longjawed orbweaver of the *Tetragnatha* genus.

73

Other tetragnathids

The golden silk orbweaver (*Nephila clavipes*) is a tropical dweller and does not live in Maine, but is worth mentioning because it spins huge orb webs of gold-colored silk. The silk has been gathered and processed to make beautiful clothing, including a garment presented to Pope Francis.

Also of interest is the fate of certain *Leucage* genus tetragnathids in Costa Rica. A parasitoid wasp (*Hymenoepimecis argyraphaga*) reproduces by attacking the spider in its web, disabling it with a paralyzing sting and then gluing an egg to its abdomen. For the next week or two, the spider goes about its business unfazed, building normal webs. Meanwhile, the egg hatches and the larva, remaining attached to the spider's body, drills tiny holes to suck hemolymph (analogously speaking, the spider's blood).

After entering its second stage of life, the larva on the night it intends to kill the spider injects a psychotropic drug that induces the spider to build a whole different kind of web out of dragline silk. This "cocoon web" has basically only radial lines that are attached differently to the surroundings, but that are more solid for holding a cocoon than the spirals of the normal orb web. The larva then molts, and that night kills and eats the spider. The next night, the larva spins a cocoon which it hangs by a line from the drug-induced web. It completes its cycles and reaches adult wasphood in a little more than a week. Studies have found that spiders saved from being killed by the larvae gradually rediscover how to build a normal orb web.

A *Leucage* spider, the orchard spider (*Leucage venusta*), has been found in Maine. The wasp, *Hymenoepimecis argyraphaga*, is found only in Costa Rica.

A longjawed orbweaver creeps along an icy sumac branch in late December.

Spiders in Winter

"Saw today a dark colored spider of the very largest kind
on ice—the Mill pond at E. Woods in Acton."
—*from H.D. Thoreau's journal, Dec. 18, 1855*

One late-December afternoon I was looking at the ice-crusted branches of the staghorn sumac in my backyard, when what to my wondering eyes should appear but a longjawed orbweaver (family Tetragnathidae) clambering along a twig in between the frozen clots.

What happens to spiders in Maine's harsh winters?

It turns out that the vast majority of spiders—about 85 percent overall—overwinter in soil and leaf litter. The rest tend to die as adults in the fall, depending on each species' life cycle and, to some extent, the climate. Spiders' life cycles are charac-

terized by five basic patterns:

- Species that mature after two or more years and overwinter in various stages of their development, including as adults (eurychronous species, in which adult spiders may be present at any time of year, such as some wolf spiders).

- Species that reproduce in spring or summer and overwinter in immature, or subadult, stages (stenochronous species, in which adults tend to be present only in certain seasons, such as cobweb weavers and jumping spiders).

- Species that lay eggs in autumn and overwinter as spiderlings in the egg case (stenochronous species, such as orbweavers).

- Species that reproduce during winter (stenochronous species such as some sheetweb weavers, which are also characterized as winter-mature).

- Species that reproduce in both spring and autumn and overwinter as adults (diplochronous species, which have two reproductive cycles per year).

Many orbweaving spiders' life cycles involve mating in summer and laying eggs in fall, with the adults dying after one season. Among the others, many overwinter in subadult or juvenile stages, and in some cases as adults. Overwintering spiders are characterized as winter-active or winter-inactive.

Winter-inactive spiders find shelter and enter diapause, a sort of hibernation state in which they draw their legs in and go stiff, with their metabolisms greatly reduced, until warmer spring weather reactivates them. Winter-active spiders, on the other hand, continue to move around and feed at temperatures below freezing (32 degrees Fahrenheit). Studies in western Canada found that the most abundant winter-active species were predominantly wolf spiders (Lycosidae), followed by sheetweb weavers (primarily

A comb-tailed spider (*Cicurina*) on ice in Fairfield, Maine. Photo by James Reben.

Erigoninae, or dwarf sheetweavers), and some species of crab spiders (Thomisidae). Other spiders known to be winter-active under litter and snow are sac spiders (Clubionidae) and longjawed orbweavers (Tetragnathidae), like the one I saw in my icy sumac.

Some of the best protection for overwintering spiders is underneath the snow pack, which works as a kind of insulation. About 8 inches of snow can maintain a fairly constant temperature of roughly 27 F underneath, even when the air temperature is as low as minus 30 F. Snow can keep a spider's leaf-litter shelter at around 32 F, and researchers have found that air temperatures as low as minus 40 F hardly affect spiders under snow.

Another way spiders withstand the cold is through a physiological adaptation called supercooling. The mechanism is not well understood, but the hemolymph (or circulating fluid analogous to mammalian blood) in some spiders contains glycerol, which in association with certain proteins acts like an antifreeze. Supercooling among spiders has been observed effective at 18 F and down to 10 F; some species of garden spider have resisted freezing to death even when exposed to cold as low as minus 4 F, and the eggs of some cobweb weavers have remained viable down to minus 40 F. Spiders in colder climates tend to have lower supercooling points than those in warmer areas; some species of thin-legged wolf spiders (*Pardosa*) in Canada are hardier in deep cold than members of the same species in Great Britain.

It's thought that for some winter-active spiders, starvation could be a survival mechanism. As the temperature dips toward the supercooling point, some spiders may cease eating because the hemolymph of some prey may not contain cryoprotectants and thus the meal can freeze in the spider's gut. So it's in the interest of the spider not to ingest freezable food in deep cold.

Some spiders ensure their species' survival by laying eggs in late summer or fall and bundling them into a silk cocoon to overwinter and then hatch in spring. Some spider eggs can remain viable in temperatures as low as minus 11 F. Cross spiders (*Araneus diadematus*) mate during late summer, and the female then spins a cocoon and lays her eggs in it. Within a few days of laying the eggs, she dies, and the spiderlings hatch out in the spring. Black-and-yellow garden spiders (*Argiope aurantia*) and barn spiders (*Araneus cavaticus*) follow a similar routine, though I watched a mother barn spider guard her egg sac for weeks before she finally died in early December.

In our part of the world, the fairly common goldenrod crab spiders (*Misumena vatia*) lay their eggs in late summer. The spiderlings hatch out in the fall, overwinter in the ground, go through a molt in May, and then spend the one full summer of their lives eating bees and producing the next batch of spiderlings.

Some species of wolf spiders mate in late summer, and then the females overwinter in ground shelters or in a building, some remaining winter-active. They spin a cocoon for their eggs in May, and the little spiders hatch in early to midsummer. The spiderlings mature relatively slowly, overwintering as subadults and then reaching adulthood the next summer. Males don't seem to live beyond the first summer of their maturity, but females may live several years.

As an overall pattern, spiders seem to favor overwintering as subadults, rather than as adults or as eggs. Spiders are so well-adapted in general to the cold that some spiders' life cycles can be longer in colder climates—in some cases extending to up to four years beyond characteristic one- or two-year cycles.

Winter mortality rates are surprisingly low for spiders. Adaptibility is the name of their game. And nature's. ✳

A house spider (*Parasteatoda*) in her web with egg sacs.

COBWEB WEAVERS
Family Theridiidae

The cobweb weavers include what might be the spider most often seen by humans, the common house spider. The teardrop shape of its abdomen is characteristic of many cobweb weavers, together with relatively long legs and fairly small chelicerae, or mouth parts. Cobweb weavers are sometimes called comb-footed spiders because they have a comb-like organ on the tarsus, or last segment, of their fourth legs, which the spider uses to bind silk around prey caught in the web.

Common house spiders are the principal builders of the space-filling webs that seem to last forever on ceilings and corners in the basement and attic. Cobweb weavers generally are comfortable spinning their webs outside, too, in sheltered places such as underneath rock faces, branches, and leaves. The webs look like, and are often described as, disorganized tangles of silk. But studies have shown that cobweb weavers engage in a definite, if variable, construction process in which the spider inspects the site, sets to work laying out structural threads, and then uses this scaffolding to expand the web with lines of silk. The webs are usually built at night, and completed gradually over a span of several days. These webs remain in place for extended periods, and undergo expansions and repairs that don't seem to be systematic, in contrast to the practices of some orbweavers.

There are all kinds of cobwebs, from just a few lines of silk to debris webs festooned with plant and bug detritus, some with retreats where the spider rests.

Some cobweb weavers, like the common house spider, spin "gumfoot webs." In this variation, the spider attaches a dragline to a supporting thread in the main web, then drops down, paying out silk on the way, and attaches the line to the ground underneath the main web. It then works its way slowly back up the thread, depositing viscid, sticky silk along the whole line. The spider usually constructs several of these gumfooted lines. When an insect encounters the line, it gets stuck, and as it flails to try to escape, the line breaks at the bottom and bungees upward, where the insect is left dangling helplessly in midair. The more the bug flails, the more entangled it gets.

While the common house spider lives comfortably and pretty conspicuously around humans, most theridiids, which includes the widow spiders, are shy and reclusive. Some of them, such as certain species of *Rhomphaea* and *Neospintharus*, both of which turn up in Maine, invade the webs of other spiders and eat their prey or even the spiders themselves. The female cobweb weaver spins an egg sac which she suspends in her tangle web and guards. She watches over the spiderlings, who live with her in the web for a short period after hatching. Cobweb weavers are thought mainly to be inactive in winter, with studies finding juveniles and adult females in winter months.

The *World Spider Catalog* in 2019 listed more than 2,500 species of cobweb weavers worldwide. It was the fourth most abundant family collected in Jennings and Graham's Milbridge study, behind wolf spiders, sheetweb weavers, and jumping spiders.

According to Cameron, the genus name *Theridion* derives from the Greek word θηριδιον (theridion, "tiny beast, animalculus"), a diminutive form of the noun θηπιον (therion, "wild beast"); it competed in use with the Latin cognate *Theridium* until the 1950s when the Greek-derived form was officially authorized in the *Official List of Generic Names in Zoology*.

A house spider.

Dipoena nigra

Dipoena nigra is an example of a tiny spider, with females around 3 mm (.11 inch) in total body length and males as small as 1.5 mm. It has been found in low vegetation and trees and on the ground. It is not known to build a capture web, and preys on small ants. Jennings and Graham found *D. nigra* in the Milbridge study, and two other species, *D. buccalis* and *D. dorsata*, also have been found in Maine, according to the early unpublished version of Jennings and Donahue's checklist of Maine spiders.

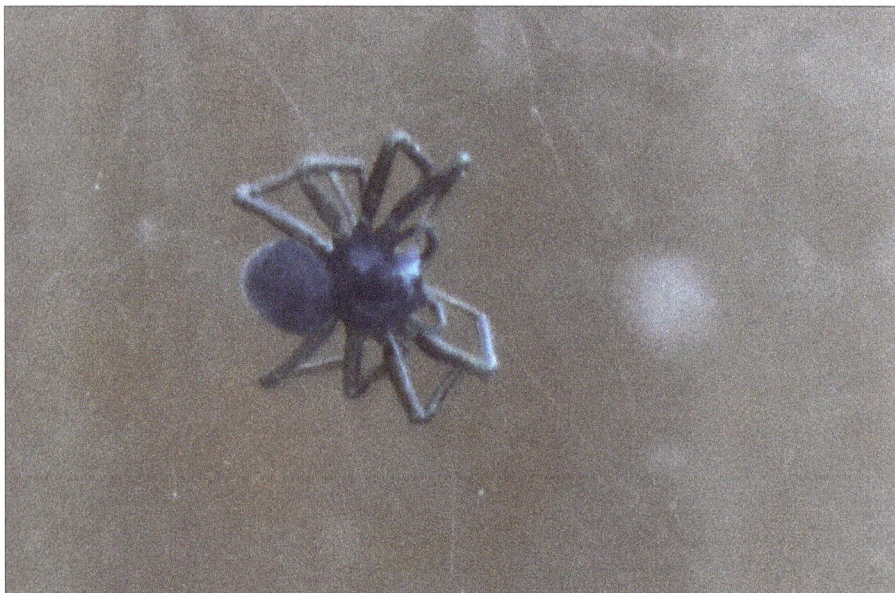

Dipoena.

Enoplognatha ovata

Enoplognatha ovata is also known unofficially as the candy stripe spider or red-and-white cobweb weaver. It lives in low brush such as milkweed or sometimes maple or ash trees, where it builds its web underneath leaves. Theridiids in general have relatively small chelicerae (mouth parts), but those of *E. ovata* males are unusually large, with long fangs.

Arachnologists who studied *E. ovata* on Mount Desert Island reported the spiders sometimes build "colonies" of webs. They lay eggs by midsummer and guard the sacs from inside the web until hatch time around September. The spiderlings disperse in the fall and overwinter in leaf litter on the ground. One study showed they can live through temperatures as low as minus 15 degrees Fahrenheit. When they emerge in spring they build small webs in the curls of dead leaves, and then as they start to molt relocate into the live brush and trees.

The candy stripe spider is "polymorphic," meaning it can have several (in this case three) different kinds of markings. The "morph" I've seen most commonly has a pale yellow abdomen with pairs of dark spots, but no stripes; this is called the lineata form. A second morph has two red stripes running the length of its abdomen; this is the redimita form. The third has a solid red band down the back of its abdomen, the ovata form. It's theorized that the different markings provide different kinds of cover from birds and other predators, involving not just camouflage but also disguise, where a bird may learn to seek a certain visual image causing it to ignore a different morph.

Enoplognatha ovata is not native to Maine and may have been introduced to both North American coasts by boat from Eurasia. It was the seventh most numerous of all species collected in the Milbridge study. Several other species of *Enoplognatha* turned up in the study, including the marbled cobweb spider (*Enoplognatha marmorata*).

Cameron says the ancient Greek formation *Enoplognatha* means, roughly, "armed jaw"—ενοπλος (enoplos, "armed") and γναθος (gnathos, "jaw"). The Latin-derived word ovata indicates "egg-shaped."

The pale yellow morph of the candy stripe spider (*Enoplognatha ovata*) on a milkweed leaf.

Neospintharus trigonum

Neospintharus trigonum, sometimes known as the dewdrop spider, is usually small and has a triangular-shaped abdomen when viewed from the side. It sometimes builds a cobweb, but also practices kleptoparasitism, meaning it steals prey from other spiders' webs; sometimes it will kill and eat the owner and take over its web.

Daniel Jennings and two other researchers, while studying the invasive sheet-web weaver *Linyphia triangularis* in Acadia National Park in the early 2000s, noticed a *N. trigonum* (known then as *Argyrodes trigonum*) eating a female *L. triangularis* in the linyphiid's own web. They soon noticed more instances of *N. trigonum* in *L. triangularis* webs and undertook a small-scale study to find out if the theridiid was indeed preying on the invasive spider. They found marauding *N. trigonum* individuals—sometimes several at a time—in *L. triangularis* webs at fairly high rates in Dixmont and Garland, and once in Milbridge.

Since *L. triangularis* is thought to have arrived in Maine only in the last three or four decades, the scientists noted that *N. trigonum* must have quickly learned to take over *L. triangularis* webs and even eat the owners. This implies *N. trigonum* is not just a creature of habit, but a flexible, adaptable theridiid. They are known to prey predominantly on the filmy dome spider (*Neriene radiata*, a sheetweb weaver) and to steal predominantly from hammock spiders (*Pityohyphantes costatus*, also a sheetweb weaver) and their theridiid cousin the common house spider (*Parasteatoda*).

The genus name *Neospintharus* is derived from the Greek word νεο (neo, "new") and Spintharus, the name of the slave and amanuensis of the Roman writer Cicero, which the 19th century naturalist Nicholas Marcellus Hentz took from a Latin dictionary, according to Cameron.

Neospintharus trigonum captured in a vial.

Neospintharus trigonum on a deck chair.

Common house spider (*Parasteatoda tepidariorum*)

The common house spider might be the most frequently noticed spider world-wide, and they are certainly conspicuously present in buildings in Maine. They have the familiar teardrop-shaped abdomens, and possibly their most notorious characteristic is the cobwebs they build in the corners of attic, cellar, shed, and garage ceilings. Their gray or brown, papery-textured egg sacs, teardrop-shaped with point up, can be seen suspended in the main web, sometimes several at the same time. After hatching, the young spiderlings remain in a group in the web for a while before dispersing.

Common house spiders probably do not overwinter outdoors in latitudes as far north as Maine, and they are less commonly seen farther north in Canada; but they may live for a couple of years inside. *Parasteatoda tepidariorum* is hard to tell apart from *Parasteatoda tabulata*, which is also seen in Maine, but about which not much research has been done so far. Before recent changes in taxonomic names, arachnologists referred to *P. tepidariorum* as *Achaearanea* and *Theridion tepidariorum*.

Above: A house spider (*Parasteatoda*).

Left: A house spider (*Parasteatoda*) with her egg sacs.

Steatoda

Steatoda spiders are in general medium-sized, with abdomens often dark-purplish to almost black with light to white markings; *S. borealis* has a reddish-brown cephalothorax with a light centerline and outline creating a T formation. They're found in a variety of habitats, including shrubs and low in trees, as well as around and sometimes in buildings. They're winter-active as adults.

Steatoda borealis, which is native to Maine, was less numerous in Jennings and Graham's Milbridge study than its very similar cousin *S. bipunctata*, an invasive species. The first collections of *S. bipunctata* were made in Nova Scotia in 1913, and until the mid-1930s *S. bipunctata* was not found outside Maine, the Maritime Provinces, and southern Québec. *Steatoda borealis* populations declined along the coast, displaced by *S. bipunctata*, but by the 1980s were persisting in forestland with minimal human presence, according to a study at the time.

Cameron explains the genus name *Steatoda* results from a series of misconstruals or misuses of the Greek στεατωδης (steatodis, "like suet") to mean fat and, by mistaken extension, rotund. Most literally construed, the name means "tallowy," according to Cameron.

Steatoda borealis.

Widow spiders (*Latrodectus*)

The Theridiidae also include the infamous widow spiders (sometimes known as hourglass spiders after the shape of the brightly colored marking underneath the abdomen), whose bite is medically significant to humans. But despite widespread fears, widow spiders rarely bite people, because like most cobweb weavers, they are relatively shy spiders that run away from danger whenever possible.

Widow spiders are not indigenous to Maine and show up only rarely. None was found in Jennings and Graham's Milbridge study of 1991-2005. The earlier unpublished version of Jennings and Donahue's checklist of Maine spiders showed two identifications of the western black widow (*Latrodectus hesperus*).

In 1988, Daniel Jennings and Ivan McDaniel reported on the discovery in Bangor in October 1986 of a female western black widow with an egg sac. The spider and the egg sac were collected, and the eggs were allowed to hatch, producing 292 spiderlings. Jennings and McDaniel determined that the spider had accidentally stowed away in the belongings of a family who had driven cross-country from Phoenix, Arizona, to Bangor that September. After the research was completed, all the spiders were killed.

The researchers said that as of the time of the report, no breeding populations of black widow spiders were known to exist in Maine, and by the late 2010s, this was still true, even though individuals are on rare occasions accidentally

This logy widow spider, probably a southern black widow (*Latrodectus mactans*) or a brown widow (*L. geometricus*), was found in Brunswick, Maine, in July 2015 when it fell from a carton that had arrived recently from Texas. The spider died soon after this photo was taken. Photo by Phil Kennedy.

brought into the state. Maine's winters overall are too cold for widow spiders to survive. But Jennings and McDaniel stated in their report that given shelter and enough warmth (about 50 degrees Fahrenheit), for example in an attic, it's possible a family of widow spiders could survive a Maine winter. Possible, but widow spiders are not known to be established in Maine.

It's worth noting that the other potentially dangerous spider of some notoriety, the brown recluse (*Loxosceles reclusa*), is not a member of family Theridiidae. It is in family Sicariidae, having only six eyes. No sicariids turned up in the Milbridge study, and none was listed in the earlier unpublished version of Jennings and Donahue's checklist of Maine spiders. The brown recluse spider's established range is in the South and southern Midwest.

The genus name *Latrodectus* is of uncertain etymological origin because of misrepresentations and mistakes in Greek grammar following the 19th century French naturalist Charles Walckenaer's naming, but according to Cameron, Walckenaer intended the invented word λατροδηκτος (*Latrodectus*) to mean "biting in secret."

Loxosceles is from an invented Greek word λοξοσκελης (loxoscelos) meaning roughly "with slanted legs."

Spiders as Predators

A fascinating scene played out in a top corner of my kitchen window one autumn, when a Western conifer seed bug became entangled in a cobweb.

The bug, naturally, struggled to get free, and the web owner, a common house spider (*Parasteatoda*), immediately picked up the vibrations and scooted down the web. She started working silk near the legs of the bug, which was four or five times as big as the spider. The conifer seed bug struggled and tried to fend off the spider with its second, longer leg. The spider quickly lashed silk near the bug's foot and then ran back along the cobweb.

In a few seconds the spider returned and, dodging the bug's kicking leg, made a few more lashings with deft movements of her front and second sets of legs, then dashed back up the web, tying off strands of silk. Sometimes she tied off a strand in one spot, sometimes made a semicircuit to several places where she worked for a few seconds and then ran back to the bug. The conifer seed bug writhed futilely, kicking at the spider, but the spider would quickly fasten a bit of silk around the end of the leg and scoot back up the web to tie it off.

This went on for quite a while. One strand of silk at a time, the spider immobilized first the longer kicking leg and then the smaller foreleg by binding them to the web.

At this point I left the scene for about two minutes to see what the cat had knocked over. When I returned, the kitchen was filled with the strong, moldy-pine-like stink of the chemical conifer seed bugs secrete in self-defense. The bug was no longer struggling. The spider, no doubt, with the bug's legs lashed fast to the web, had bitten the bug with her side-to-side jaws and injected paralyzing venom through the tips of her fangs.

The spider had retreated to the other corner of the window. I assume she stayed there until the bug was completely paralyzed. Then she would start to eat.

A house spider (*Parasteatoda*) subdues a deer fly.

The next day the conifer seed bug was hanging upside down farther up the web. Cobweb weavers (family Theridiidae), such as the house spider and the widow spiders, make an incision in the bug's body, into which they spew enzymes that pre-digest tissue. The spider's stomach then acts like a pump, sucking the digested material into the spider's mouth and down its gut. The spider's usual routine is to regurgitate the digestive enzymes many times, sort of bite by bite. Goldenrod crab spiders, for another example, use the same technique as the theridiids, piercing the prey with two tiny holes through which they predigest the bug's insides, then draw out the fluid. The remains of their meals are usually hollowed-out corpses.

Other spiders, notably orbweavers, use their fangs to tear apart their prey, spewing the digestive enzymes over the bug part by part, usually leaving an unrecognizable lump of non-comestible flesh afterward.

The spider ingests only soft material that its body can absorb. Any hard particles that do not get pre-digested (especially among spiders that first tear their prey apart) are filtered by hairs around the spider's mouth and by platelets in the pharynx. Strange as it may sound, after a meal the spider washes up by using its palps to clean debris from its mouth and hair.

Studies indicate that spiders can taste their food: researchers in the 1930s observed that spiders discriminated between clear water and a weak solution of quinine.

The house spider probably got several meals out of the conifer seed bug. Spiders by and large eat only living tissue (or at any rate, things they kill themselves). The arachnologists don't have a way of figuring out how long the bug may have lived after receiving the paralyzing bite. I once watched a goldenrod crab spider muckle onto the face of a bee and hold it for more than an hour while it sucked the insides out of the bee's head. This conifer seed bug, meanwhile, provided feasts to this house spider for three days, until one morning the hollowed-out body had been cut loose from the web and was lying on the window sill.

Predator

It has been estimated that spiders kill between 400 million and 800 million tons of prey every year worldwide, and that each year they eat 105,840 pounds of insects for every 2 acres of North American forestland. They secure their food by an incredible array of methods, from ambushing and stalking, to web snares, to, in the case of bolas spiders, using silk like a bolo line to snag moths in flight. Some are kleptoparasites who steal other animals' catches. All but one family of spiders (Uloboridae, the hackled orbweavers, which subdue by wrapping in silk) produce venom which they in-

A banded garden spider wraps up a captured dragonfly.

ject into prey through the tips of their jaws, paralyzing the catch.

Spiders' diet consists mostly of insects, as well as other small arthropods such as springtails and even other spiders. A very few specialize in ants, though most spiders avoid them. Fishing spiders (Pisauridae) and some wolf spiders (Lycosidae) sometimes eat small vertebrates such as minnows, tadpoles, or frogs. A fishing spider, for example, will sit with six of its legs stretched out on the surface of a pond or stream, awaiting the vibrations of minnows which it dives down to snatch and then drag to shore or onto a lily pad. Some crab spiders (Thomisidae) drink nectar from plant blossoms.

Spiders seldom suffer from starvation, in part because they can sur-

A cobweb weaver ties up a captured army worm.

vive weeks and more without eating, and in part because they are generalists, meaning that when certain populations of insects become scarce, the spiders simply move on to others that are more abundant. ✳

A longlegged sac spider (*Cheiracanthium*).

Hunters

SAC SPIDERS
Family Clubionidae

The sac spiders are nocturnal hunters that patrol mainly on plants and bark and under leaf litter and rocks. Like the ground spiders (family Gnaphosidae), they don't build a capture web, but they do build a tubular or saclike retreat, often in rolled leaves, where they rest during the day, molt, and deposit their egg sacs. One way to distinguish a sac spider from a ground spider is to note the conical-shaped, close-set spinnerets on the abdomen; ground spiders' spinnerets are often more prominently visible and distinctly separate and cylindrical in shape.

Many sac spiders overwinter in their "penultimate" instars, or next to last stage of maturity, with the males dying out by early summer (after mating, presumably) and the female adults living through the summer. Some sac spiders, such as *Clubiona* (also known as leafcurling sac spiders) and *Cheiracanthium* (reclassified from Clubionidae to Cheiracanthiidae, see below), may find their way into your house for the winter.

The *World Spider Catalog* in 2019 indicated there are more than 630 species of Clubionidae worldwide. Jennings and Graham identified individuals from 13

A leafcurling sac spider (*Clubiona*).

A sac spider patrolling the kitchen counter.

A sac spider.

species (in the categories used around 2002) in the Milbridge study. The family has been undergoing considerable changes to its membership, as arachnologists continue to work out the taxonomy, or categories of spiders. Whole subfamilies and groups of two-clawed spiders have been moved around between families Clubionidae, Cheiracanthiidae (longlegged sac spiders), Corinnidae (antmimic spiders), Gnaphosidae (ground spiders), Liocranidae (spinylegged sac spiders), and Miturgidae (prowling spiders), among others, all of which have been found in Maine.

While almost no spiders are dangerous to humans, the longlegged sac spider (sometimes called the yellow sac spider, genus *Cheiracanthium*) is said to sometimes administer a painful, but not dangerous bite. (*Cheiracanthium* was recently recategorized to family Cheiracanthiidae (synonymous with Eutichuridae), after occupying Miturgidae and before that Clubionidae.) Two species of *Cheiracanthium* have been documented in Maine, according to the earlier unpublished version of Jennings and Donahue's checklist of Maine spiders; none were recorded in Jennings and Graham's Milbridge study.

The origin of the name Clubionidae has been a matter of speculation among arachnologists since the 19th century, according to Cameron. The French naturalist Pierre André Latreille invented the genus name *Clubiona* in 1804, but from what words, it's not clear. Cameron accepts the finding of Swedish arachnologist Tamerlan Thorell, later in the 19th century, quoting him as saying, "'Perhaps the name is formed from κλωβιον (kloubion), a bird-trap (with reference to the sack-like tube which these spiders inhabit).'"

This redspotted antmimic (*Castianeira descripta*) was found darting around in a garden in Fairfield, Maine. Photo by James Reben.

A twobanded antmimic (*Castianeira cingulata*) in Fairfield, Maine. Photo by James Reben.

ANTMIMIC SPIDERS

Family Corinnidae

Many species of Corinnidae resemble ants, hence the name antmimic spiders. Most in the Maine area live on the ground among leaf litter in woods and fields, as well as bogs. They move quickly, like ants, and are hunters who do not build snares. Some species are nocturnal, while others, mainly those who most strikingly resemble ants, are diurnal. Some species have been found living around ants, an unusual arrangement because ants have potent and variegated defenses against predators, and many insects and spiders avoid them. Adult females of the two-banded antmimic species (*Castianeira cingulata*) can be found year round, overwintering in thick silk sacs that they spin in sheltered places such as rock crevices and inside decayed wood.

The Corinnidae make up one of the families that have been undergoing frequent taxonomic changes, with a number of genera and species being shifted around among the Gnaphosidae (ground spiders), Clubionidae (sac spiders), and Liocranidae (spinylegged sac spiders) families. In Jennings and Graham's Milbridge study published in 2002, eight species of antmimic spiders were represented, including the two-banded antmimic (*Castianeira cingulata*) and the redspotted antmimic (*C. descripta*), pictured here.

The name of the *Corinna* genus of antmimic spiders was derived by the 19th century naturalist C.L. Koch from the name of the sixth century B.C. Greek lyric poet Corinna. No spiders of the *Corinna* genus are known to make their home in Maine; the town of Corinna in Penobscot County is not named for the spider or the poet, but after the daughter of the town's founder.

This jumping spider somehow lost two of its legs and was hobbling around on just six.

Spiders as Prey

Like every other creature, spiders are subject to a variety of dangers, including getting eaten, infected, and injured.

Most spiders are generalist predators who are dangerous not only to bugs, but to each other. Pirate spiders, aka cannibal spiders (family Mimetidae), for example, eat only other spiders. Members of the *Ero* genus, two species of which have been identified in Maine, trick some orb-weaving spiders by plucking dragline silk in imitation of courtship signals. When the female leaves the web, *Ero* attacks, often biting a leg. Some wandering spiders attack each other as part of the hunt,

and some spiders invade webs and subdue and eat the owner.

Some insects prey regularly on spiders, including some ants; certain kinds of flies, such as mantidflies, attack and eat spider eggs, and some kinds of wasps in particular prey on spiders. Mud dauber wasps go right into a spider's web and, using "aggressive mimicry," trick the spider by plucking the silk and then attacking when the spider investigates. Spider wasps (family Pompilidae) pursue only spiders, and have methods of knocking orb weavers, for example, out of their webs to the ground, grappling them with their forelegs

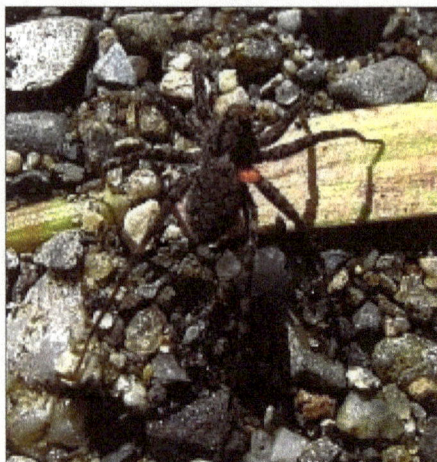

This thin-legged wolf spider (*Pardosa*) is plagued by mites, the bright red spots visible at its midsection.

This sac spider (family Clubionidae) is suffering from a parasite, probably a pompilid wasp larva, visible where its pedicel meets its abdomen.

and mandibles, and then paralyzing them with a sting. They drag the paralyzed spider into a hole, where they may store them to eat weeks later. Most spiders appear to be terrified of spider wasps and try to run away, although researchers have seen some wolf spiders try to push the wasp away or hide behind a plug of sand; hackledmesh weavers of the *Amaurobius* genus seem unfazed by pompilids and sometimes will overpower and eat an attacking wasp when it gets entangled in the hackledmesh web.

Spiders are part of the diet of some vertebrate animals, including toads, lizards, and fish, especially trout, which seize them from the water surface. Birds are known to eat spiders in some abundance in winter and spring, but scientists have not nailed down exactly what effect birds have on spider populations. Many spiders are well-concealed visually, either by their shape and coloration or by holding still in their webs, and many are nocturnal, adaptations that serve as significant foils to birds' keen eyesight.

Other perils

Spiders also may be attacked by parasites. Wasps, again, can be a major danger. The life cycle of some ichneumon wasps includes laying eggs on a spider's body, or in the case of some wolf spiders, in their egg sacs, where the larvae feed after hatching out. Some species of spider wasps subdue the spider with a sting, then lay an egg on it and depart, while others drag the spider to a selected location, dig a hole, position the spider inside, and then lay an egg on its body. When the egg hatches after a few days, the wasp larva eats the paralyzed spider alive.

The larvae of spider flies (family Acroceridae, a kind of true flies) attach themselves to a spider's leg, then crawl onto the abdomen and penetrate into the body near the spider's book lung, where they live and feed on the spider's insides for months or, in the case of some tarantulas, years. Some kinds of tachinid flies also internally parasitize spiders.

Many spiders also suffer from roundworm (nematode) parasites. One species of mermithid roundworm lays its eggs in water, where they're swallowed by an insect, such as a yellow-jacket, and live out the next phase of life in the insect's body. They remain dormant through the insect's maturation process, then when the insect is captured and eaten by a spider, the roundworm larvae activate and parasitize the spider. Roundworms grow to adulthood in the spider's body and eventually emerge, usually through a ventral opening.

Mites can also plague the outside of spiders' bodies. Not all mites that ride spiders are parasitic, but some attach larvae along the edge or side of the spider's pedicel and cephalothorax, where they feed on the spider.

Spiders can also succumb to infections of entomophagous (or insect-eating) fungi. This occurs mostly in tropical and subtropical areas, and has been observed in North Carolina. Sheetweb weavers have been found dead amid entomophagous fungi in the Arctic.

In addition to dangers from predators and parasites, spiders also suffer injuries during the course of everyday spider life. It's estimated that about 75 percent of spiders lose one or two legs at some point in their lives as a result of fights, accidents, an awkward molt in which the exoskeleton doesn't drop off cleanly and a leg gets pinned, or even during rough mating when a male is attacked by a female. Spiders missing one leg or even several can still make webs; researchers observed a spider missing five legs awkwardly but successfully spin an orb web.

Most spiders can amputate an injured leg, an operation called autotomy. Running crab spiders and cellar spiders seem to amputate their own legs quite readily, while others, such as jumping spiders and crab spiders, seem to do so only as a last resort. Some long-jawed orb-weavers apparently never autotomize.

Most juvenile spiders can regenerate a lost leg in their next molt, if the loss occurs in the early stage of the intermolt phase. Adult spiders can't regenerate a lost leg, since they don't molt again. ✳

A parson spider (*Herpyllus ecclesiasticus*) on the deck rail. The yellow corpse just in front of the spider may be a prey item; the lines that seem to be swirling around are probably hair, as well as silk strands that originated from a different spider; ground spiders normally do not make much silk as they move around.

GROUND SPIDERS

Family Gnaphosidae

Ground spiders, sometimes known as mouse spiders, live mainly under leaf litter and rocks, and some species have found advantages in living alongside humans inside buildings. They're wandering hunters who stalk their prey, and most are nocturnal. They use their silk to make egg sacs (which the females of many species guard until they hatch) and draglines, and many build a tubular retreat under rocks or in a rolled leaf where they rest during the day. One clue to identifying a ground spider is the presence of cone-shaped spinnerets that are widely separated and protrude prominently from the back of the abdomen.

Being hunters, ground spiders' eyesight is quite good. Not only do they need to spot their prey, but they also need to find their way back to the retreat in the morning, and studies have shown that the eyes of *Drassodes* genus ground spiders are equipped to distinguish angles of polarized light, which they read at dawn and dusk to navigate back home. (*Drassodes neglectus* is found in Maine.) Some species of wolf spiders (family Lycosidae, also hunters) have a similar visual capability, though their eye anatomy differs from *Drassodes'* anatomy, probably giving different visual experiences to the different spiders. Human eyes tend to experience polarizations of light as glare, but many birds, insects, and spiders distinguish polarizations.

Micaria species of Gnaphosidae are what's known as ant mimics. They look like ants and can be found among them during the day. Jennings and Graham list three *Micaria* species in the Milbridge study. (The main ant mimic family of spiders is Corinnidae.)

Many species of ground spiders overwinter in leaf litter as subadults. They are categorized by some researchers as "winter inactive," meaning they tend to enter diapause, or hibernate, and some species, at least, spin silk cocoons where they wait out the cold weather.

There are more than 2,500 identified species of Gnaphosidae, according to the *World Spider Catalog* in 2019, the seventh most numerous spider family worldwide. Jennings and Graham turned up 17 species in their Milbridge study, and it was the eighth most numerous family found.

The genus name *Gnaphosa* has a murky background, according to Cameron, with possible origins in the biblical word γνοφος (gnophos, "darken"). "It is clear Latreille [who assigned the first names to this genus] intended the name to mean 'living in the dark,'" he says.

Parson spider (*Herpyllus ecclesiasticus*)

A noticeable ground spider found in Maine is the parson spider, *Herpyllus ecclesiasticus*, which operates under stones on the forest floor, sometimes in buildings, and occasionally in low vegetation. Young parson spiders overwinter under bark. These spiders run surprisingly fast and are capable of "astonishing maneuvers," as one guidebook puts it.

The name parson derives from the long, white chevron-like marking on *H. ecclesiasticus*'s cephalothorax, which has been described as resembling a minister's necktie. The genus name *Herpyllus* may be related to the Greek ερπυλλος (erpullos, "tufted thyme") in association with the verb ερπω (erpo, "to crawl"), according to Cameron.

A wolf spider.

WOLF SPIDERS

Family Lycosidae

Wolf spiders are recognizable by their two large, front-facing eyes set over a straight row of four smaller eyes. They hunt in a wide array of habitats, such as fields, leaf litter, mossy areas, and sandy and rocky shores. They range in size from very small (2.2 mm, or .09 inch) to as large as 35 mm (nearly 1½ inches) in body length. Wolf spiders use both stalking and sit-and-wait hunting methods in leaf litter and brush, sometimes wrestling their insect prey or even another spider into submission and then biting it with unusually powerful jaws. Some are active mainly at night or twilight, others during the day.

As hunters, wolf spiders have exceptionally good eyesight through their six front-facing eyes; two smaller eyes set back on the cephalothorax enable them to detect motion to the sides and rear. The two large eyes in some lycosids provide as sharp an image as those seen by many jumping spiders, whose extraordinary eyesight has been studied extensively. *Rabidosa rabida* (a huge wolf spider not usually seen in Maine) uses its keen vision to hunt fireflies. Research has shown that some wolf spiders navigate their surroundings by detecting polarizations of light. At night, if you're in the right place with a flashlight or the moon throwing rays in just the right direction, it's possible to spot a wolf spider's eyes reflecting little green pinpricks of light.

Almost no species of wolf spiders build capture webs, but they all use silk to make draglines for navigation and in mating routines. Female wolf spiders spin egg sacs, which they carry around fixed to the spinnerets. When the spiderlings hatch, they climb on the mother's back, and she carries them around for as much as a couple of weeks, until they're ready to go hunting on their own.

Some wolf spiders are among the very few spiders whose jaws are strong enough to break human skin (others include some sac spiders, some jumping spiders, and some cobweb weavers). But with only a tiny handful of exceptions in North America, a bite by almost all of these species is not dangerous; it might not even be noticed, unless you have an allergic reaction to the venom that in unusual cases can produce a typical itching, swelling, bug-bite type wound.

The wolf spiders are among the most numerous in North America. The *World Spider Catalog* in 2019 listed more than 2,400 species of wolf spider worldwide; and they were by far the most numerous family collected in Jennings and Graham's Milbridge study.

The family name Lycosidae comes from Greek λνκοζ (lycos, "wolf"), a description for spiders of uncertain species that dates as far back as ancient Greece, according to Cameron.

Above: A wolf spider mother carrying her brood on her back. The spiderlings had hatched just a few hours before this photo was taken.

Left: This huge wolf spider, *Rabidosa rabida* which is unusual in Maine, walked out from behind a stack of school notebooks.

Wolf spider (*Pardosa*) mother with her egg sac.

This wolf spider mother fell when the photographer accidentally severed the silk dragline she was using to cling to the underside of a railing. She crashed to the deck, scattering the spiderlings (seen in background and climbing her legs) who were on her back. She was stunned and possibly injured, but may have survived, as a half hour later she had disappeared from the scene of the accident.

A wolf spider with shining eyes.

A juvenile wolf spider on Queen Anne's lace. "Will you walk into my parlour?" said the Spider to the Fly. / "'Tis the prettiest little parlour that ever you did spy."

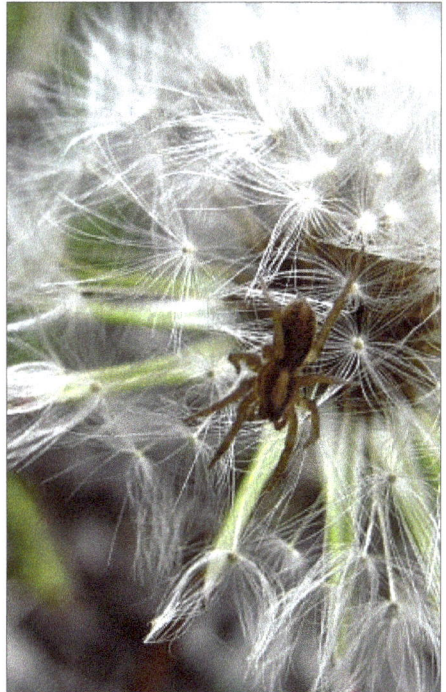

A juvenile wolf spider on a dandelion.

103

Thin-legged wolf spider (*Pardosa*)

Daniel Jennings, when I asked him a few years ago what spider might be the most common in Maine, paused a moment, then said, "Maybe *Pardosa*," the thin-legged wolf spider. Among all the spider species collected in Jennings and Graham's Milbridge study, *Pardosa moesta* was the most numerous, and *Pardosa modica* was second. *Pardosa moesta* is one of the very few in this genus that can be confidently recognized on sight, especially on beaches where they dart from place to place on their thin legs. Otherwise, distinguishing species of *Pardosa* normally requires a microscope and a key to spider anatomy.

Thin-legged wolf spiders tend to have flat, pug faces and occur on the ground in many habitats, from gravel to marshes. A study in Manitoba found that *P. moesta* and *P. distincta* (which was also abundant in the Milbridge study) overwinter as juveniles and are winter-active, meaning they move around and feed in temperatures below freezing, largely under the snow. The study found *P. fuscula* (also found in Maine) to be winter-inactive, meaning those spiders that survive winter do not move around or feed in the cold and their metabolic rates slow significantly.

The genus name *Pardosa* is derived from the Latin (pardus) and Greek (παρδοσ, pardos) for leopard, which like the spider is a predator. The last element, -osa, became a family-specific rhyming convention for lycosid genera, including for example *Alopecosa*, *Arctosa*, *Gladicosa*, *Gnaphosa*, *Schizocosa*, *Trebacosa*, *Trochosa*, and *Varecosa*, species of all of which are found in Maine.

A thin-legged wolf spider (*Pardosa*) in Augusta, Maine.

A thin-legged wolf spider (*Pardosa*) carrying her egg sac in her spinnerets.

Schizocosa

Wolf spiders of the *Schizocosa* genus are medium-sized to large spiders, usually two-toned brown or tan, sometimes with gray, in color. The size and color patterns of *Trochosa* are similar to those of nursery-web spiders (*Pisaurina mira*); *Trochosa* has the lighter band along the top of the abdomen, while the nursery-web spider has the darker band along the top. They tend to live around woodlands, often found patrolling in ground litter and sometimes around the edges of salt marshes, as found in the Milbridge study. *Schizocosa* overwinters in leaf and woods litter as subadults, and in some species as adults.

Most numerous among *Schizocosa* species in Jennings and Donahue's uncompleted list are *S. communis*, *S. crassipalpata*, and *S. saltatrix*, all three also listed in Jennings and Graham's Milbridge study. In Jennings' 1980s study of lowbush blueberry fields in Washington County, *S. communis* and the thin-legged wolf spiders *Pardosa distincta* and *P. moesta* were the most commonly found spiders.

The genus name *Schizocosa*, like *Pardosa* and *Trochosa*, was fashioned to rhyme with other lycosid genus names. According to Cameron, the first part of the word comes from Greek σχιζω (schizo, "to split"), referring to the shape of the epigynum (external part of the female sexual organs, located underneath the abdomen) which in *Schizocosa* females has the appearance of a "split T."

Schizocosa.

Trochosa

Trochosa terricola is a pretty commonly seen, large wolf spider in Maine, with the cephalothorax often a brown color with light and dark bands. *Trochosa terricola* is one of the wolf spiders whose eyes you can see shining at night, but interestingly, adult individuals of this species having no eyes have been captured, suggesting other senses are also important to hunting among wolf spiders. *Trochosa terricola* adults are active in winter.

Trochosa ruricola, which Jennings and Graham reported finding abundantly near the shore of Narraguagus Bay, was in the top 10 most numerous species collected in the Milbridge study. It's a species of wolf spider not native to Maine and could be a threat to displace *T. terricola* on offshore islands.

The genus name *Trochosa* is lifted directly from the Greek word τροχωσα (trochosa, "running quickly") partly because it makes a nice rhyme with *Lycosa*, according to Cameron.

Trochosa on patrol in sphagnum moss.

A young crab spider tiptoes in preparation to go ballooning.

Spiders in Flight

On a breezy, sunny May afternoon I was walking around the Unity park when I noticed two women peering at the back of a bench near the road. I thought this was kind of weird because usually I'm the one exhibiting odd peering behavior, usually while looking for bridge orbweavers in the genus *Larinioides*, who find the sheltered backs of those benches a perfect place for webs.

It turned out the two women had come upon a gaggle of young wolf spiders running back and forth along the bench.

"We're covered in cobwebs!" one of the women exclaimed.

And sure enough, you could see glints of silk flapping in the breeze and strands lying on the bench, on the new grass and the walking track, and trailing off the women's clothes.

The wolf spiderlings were ballooning—throwing silk onto the wind and using it like a kite to fly off to points unknown.

Since spiders have no wings, many use this technique to fly. They find an open perch, such as a tip of grass or the back of a park bench on a breezy day. Some of them then stand on tiptoe facing the wind, angle their backsides at 45 degrees, and throw threads of silk into the breeze. This is what the wolf spiderlings at the park appeared to be doing. Other species lay down a silk dragline, which they hold onto, and when a stiff enough breeze takes hold, the dragline breaks, a fray of silk balloons into the wind, and off the spiders go. Others loop threads of silk to make what amounts to a little kite, and when the breeze catches it, they take off.

Wolf spiders getting ready to go ballooning.

Ballooning spiders fly as high as 200 feet, and aircraft crews have spotted squadrons of flying spiders as high as 14,000 feet. Charles Darwin wrote that his ship the *Beagle* encountered a huge crowd of ballooning spiders 60 miles out to sea, off South America. It's thought that some species of longjawed orbweavers and crab spiders colonized remote islands by ballooning hundreds of miles across the Pacific Ocean. Because of this aeronautic adventuring, spiders are often the first arthropods to set up shop after natural disasters such as fires, mudslides, and floods.

Spiders can control their flight to some extent by changing body posture, slowing descent by splaying their legs and increasing speed by tucking the legs in. But as far as anyone knows, they have no control over where they end up. The wind decides their fate. It's thought that most don't survive long voyages because they get eaten on the fly by birds such as swallows or swifts, or they come to rest on water where they drown or get snapped up by another predator such as a fish. If they survive a landing in an inhospitable environment, they try another flight.

The aerodynamics of ballooning are not fully understood. Most ballooning takes place in the late spring or early fall, at least in part because weather conditions are conducive then. Sharply rising ground temperature can cause updrafts that the spiders can use to get airborne. One

A wolf spider ready to go ballooning.

study indicated spiders can detect electric fields that build up around objects such as grass, trees, and fences, providing electrostatic conditions the spider can use to help it get airborne. Young spiders are most commonly seen ballooning because they're small and light, but researchers have observed even some large adults, particularly among sheetweb weavers, taking off.

The most active balloonists in the vicinity of Maine are the sheetweb weavers (family Linyphiidae), notably the tiny dwarf spiders (subfamily Erigoninae). But some species of orbweavers, crab spiders, jumping spiders, longjawed orbweavers, and nursery web spiders, as well as some wolf spiders, also go ballooning.

In the park, the little wolf spiders, who are also hunters, were eagerly getting a head start on their summer-long lives. Strands of silk were everywhere, floating off the bench in the wind and getting all over my clothes. I've never seen it happen, but when the group of balloonists is really large in a field, there's so much silk that it collects together in sheets, and makes what we call gossamer—the material of the gown worn by Emily Dickinson's character who is kindly given a carriage ride by Death. ✳

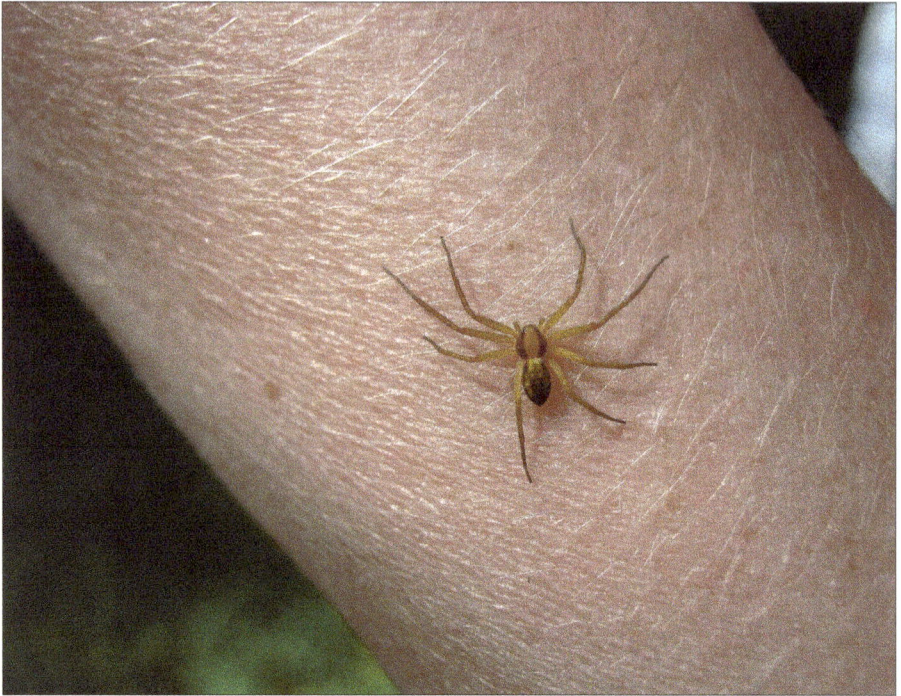

A running crab spider (*Philodromus*) on a sunlit arm.

RUNNING CRAB SPIDERS
Family Philodromidae

Running crab spiders are mainly medium-sized gray or light brown spiders. They resemble crab spiders (family Thomisidae), as they hold their front legs so the front surface is on top (a laterigrade position), making a bowlike appearance. Running crab spiders can be tricky to distinguish from crab spiders, but their eye patterns differ and in general both parts of running crab spiders' bodies are more elongated and flatter, and their second pair of slender legs are generally longer than the other three pairs.

Running crab spiders can be seen resting on smooth surfaces such as leaves, plant stems, or steel (such as cars), where they are hunting. I've found them in the mailbox. They tend to choose resting places that match their colors, facilitating camouflage against predators. They're in the informal category of wandering spiders, similar to wolf spiders and sac spiders, which move very quickly in aggressive pursuit of prey rather than ambushing (from the hunting method called sit-and-wait, as practiced by many crab spiders) or stalking (by jumping spiders or nursery web spiders). Some researchers have said that running crab spiders are one of only three spider groups that are true active-search predators, as opposed to spiders that incorporate both stalking and sit-and-wait strategies into their foraging; the other two are the jumping spiders (family Salticidae) and the *Loxosceles*, or recluse spiders (family Sicariidae). Recluse spiders, whose bite can be dangerous, are not native to Maine and are almost never seen here.

Most running crab spiders overwinter in a subadult stage, sometimes in loose groups or "pseudoflocks," as Jennings describes them. One guidebook notes they have been seen active on the snow surface on mild winter days. They tend to reach maturity in early spring.

The *World Spider Catalog* in 2019 listed more than 530 species of philodromids worldwide; 13 species were found in the Milbridge study.

The genus name *Philodromus*, devised early in the 19th century, comes from the Greek adjective φιλοδρομοσ (philodromos, "loving the course," referring to racing).

Above: A running crab spider on a wall.

Left: A running crab spider (*Philodromus marxi*) on a hubcap.

A female nursery web spider (*Pisaurina mira*).

NURSERY WEB SPIDERS AND FISHING SPIDERS
Family Pisauridae

Nursery web spiders and fishing spiders are wandering hunters with similarities to wolf spiders (family Lycosidae). They are generally fairly large spiders, rarely building snares or retreats. Unlike wolf spiders, who are usually found on the ground, nursery web spiders tend to patrol in trees and vegetation; fishing spiders hunt near water. A readily recognizable distinction between Pisauridae and Lycosidae is their eyes: pisaurids have two rows of eyes, all of about the same size, while wolf spiders' eyes are arranged in three rows with two large eyes facing front.

Nursery web spiders, fittingly enough, construct silk nurseries for their young. The females carry the egg sac under their bodies, holding it in place with a little silk and their chelicerae (mouth parts) and palps (small handlike appendages in front of the spider's face). When the eggs are near ready to hatch, she builds a tent-like nursery in vegetation, often under a folded-over leaf, where she deposits the eggs and then stands guard for a week or so while the spiderlings eclose (emerge from the egg), go through one molt, and then disperse. The brood is usually produced around midsummer in our range, and they overwinter inactively as juveniles.

A fishing spider (*Dolomedes*) on the kitchen floor.

Nursery web spiders' vision appears to be relatively good for spiders in general, but perhaps not as good as other hunters, such as wolf spiders and jumping spiders. They detect motion well, but rely to a large extent on vibrations, such as a fly buzz, to locate and run down prey. Fishing spiders, which hunt near, on, and in water, can read the vibratory differences between waves set up by breezes and waves set up by insects and fish.

The *World Spider Catalog* listed more than 350 species of nursery web and fishing spiders in 2019. In Maine five species are found in two genera: *Pisaurina* (nursery web spiders) and *Dolomedes* (fishing spiders). They were the family with the fewest individuals collected in Jennings and Graham's Milbridge study.

Nursery web spider (*Pisaurina mira*)

We frequently see *Pisaurina mira* in central Maine, patrolling on the deck in the summer and, in the spring especially, on window screens and the kitchen counter. They are unmistakably large, with females up to 16 mm (more than ½ inch) in body length with long legs that the spider often stretches out in front and back while resting. What appears to be a species variation in our range has rich tan and brown markings, a "beautiful morph," as Dr. Jerome Rovner described a photo I sent to him. *Pisaurina mira* hunts actively during much of the day, but sits quietly at times, as part of its routine.

The size and color patterns of nursery web spiders are similar to those of wolf spiders of *Trochosa* genus; *Trochosa* has the lighter band along the top of the abdomen, while the nursery web spider has the darker band along the top.

Pisaurina mira until recently was not documented for Maine in the American Arachnological Society's inventory of spiders and does not appear for Maine in Dondale and Redner's *Insects and Arachnids of Canada* (1990), Part 17 covering Lycosidae, Pisauridae, and Oxyopidae.

A male nursery web spider (*Pisaurina mira*), Maine morph.

Mating among Pisaurids

Our common species of nursery web spider practices a remarkable courtship and mating process.

Like the males of many spider species, the *Pisaurina mira* male wanders around until he detects the silk dragline of a female. He then follows the silk, pausing cautiously for short periods and raising one of his front legs. As long as she keeps watching, he slowly approaches, and the pauses become longer. At some point the female might decide she doesn't like him and runs off to some inaccessible spot.

If she decides she likes him, she allows him close enough to gently touch her hind legs with his front legs. After some leg interplay, she scoots to an apparently predetermined mating spot and attaches a dragline. He quickly follows her and takes up a position behind and over her. She then dangles freely on the dragline. He follows, and using his palps carefully turns her over. While he's doing this, he folds her legs in and binds them with a "veil of silk," as the researchers describe it.

Cradling her in his legs, he positions himself so he can reach around her body with his palps, where sperm is stored. With his left palp, he gently places sperm into her epigynum opening. He then repositions and repeats the insertion with his right palp. This happens a few times until the female gets restless. He then releases her, adding a little more binding to the veil and retreating to a safe distance. The female, still dangling, frees herself from the silken bonds. Soon she'll be carrying around an egg sac in her palps and jaws (or chelicerae). Very few spider species are known to bind the female with silk during copulation, but it serves at least partly to protect the male from being attacked and consumed.

Pisaurina mira's European cousin, *Pisaura mirabilis*, has a slightly different approach to mating. The male often first catches a bug, such as a fly, usually wrapping it in silk, and then, holding it in his chelicerae, he presents it to the female as a gift. If the female decides to receive him, she moves slowly toward him. He then raises the gift in his palps and leans backward. At some point, the female grabs the gift. Occasionally she makes off with it without copulating, but usually the male maintains a grip on the gift with his legs and a line of silk. He positions himself over her back, and while she's eating, he commences the reach-around copulation with his palps. The longer copulation lasts, the more sperm can be transferred.

Sometimes the female interrupts the copulation. When this happens, the whole session might end with the male making a hasty retreat. He might also play dead, which arachnologists call "thanatosis"; it's probably a strategy to prolong copulation as well as to avoid being eaten, though it's not known for sure. Among nursery web spiders, sexual cannibalism, as it's called, happens about 2 to 4 percent of the time and almost always before copulation, which accounts at least partly for the males' ginger approach. But it's been known to happen afterward, and researchers observed one nursery web male eaten during copulation. He had brought no gift. Giftless males in studies were by far less successful in mating than gift-bearing males.

Love and death in Dolomedes

Fishing spiders' mating procedures also have a remarkable outcome.

In most spider species, the female is larger than the male. While in most *Dolomedes* species the males are about the same size as the females, *Dolomedes tenebrosus* females, the striking exception, may weigh as much as 14 times more than the male. In their mating process, the *D. tenebrosus* male approaches the female cautiously, as do many male spiders, and when he is accepted, mounts her, and proceeds with copulation by reaching to her epigynum with his sperm-engorged palp. But toward the completion of the transfer of sperm, the male curls in his legs and becomes inert. He remains in this position for up to 25 minutes, and then dies

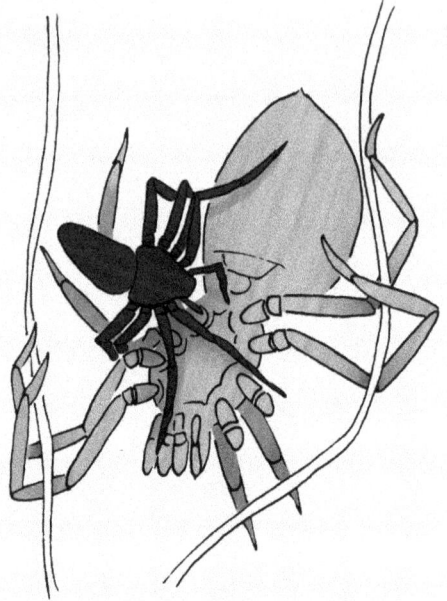

Dolomedes tenebrosus pair copulating. Illustration by Chelsea Ellis.

when the female bites his abdomen and then eats him.

This happened every time in one study. In addition, about 25 percent of *D. tenebrosus* females ate the male before the copulation. Sexual cannibalism is not usual among spiders, but not unheard of. But the females' consumption of the males in every mating interaction among the *D. tenebrosus* fishing spiders is very unusual.

What evolutionary purpose sexual cannibalism serves is not certain. One theory is that the male sacrifices himself to the female to ensure she is satiated and therefore less likely to take a second mate, ensuring that the first male's genes are passed on. ✳

Fishing spider (*Dolomedes*)

Four species of fishing spiders (*Dolomedes*, sometimes known as wharf, dock, or raft spiders) are found in Maine: *D. triton* (also known as the six-spotted fishing spider), *D. scriptus*, *D. striatus*, and *D. tenebrosus*. They are semi-aquatic spiders, meaning they spend a good deal of their lives hunting near, on, and in water. They sometimes wander into human habitations, too, and can cause a stir because of their size—they are perhaps the largest spiders native to Maine. I've found them on door frames and one night woke to see a huge female *D. tenebrosus* on the bedroom wall a few inches from my face. Females can be up to 26 mm (more than in inch) in body length. They are generally brown or light brown spiders, many with horizontal or chevron-like darker and lighter markings. *Dolomedes scriptus* can have violin-shaped markings similar to those of the brown recluse (*Loxosceles*) which is almost never found in Maine.

Fishing spiders often hunt on the shore of a pond or slow-moving stream, sometimes overhanging the water on silk. They watch for motion and listen for air and water vibrations to detect prey, which consist not only of flying, ground, and aquatic insects, but sometimes even vertebrates such as minnows and tadpoles. Many web-weaving, crab, and jumping spiders cannot walk on

A fishing spider (*Dolomedes tenebrosus*) climbing the cellar doorframe.

A fishing spider (*Dolomedes*) with a moth victim.

water, but fishing spiders, along with some wolf spiders (family Lycosidae) and longjawed orbweavers (family Tetragnathidae), can. The *Dolomedes* spiders use a kind of rowing motion with their middle pairs of legs. When a burst of speed is needed to run down an insect or escape a predator, they kick into a sort of galloping stride across the surface of the water, covering up to 20 inches very quickly. Some of them also use their bodies to catch a breeze and sail across the water.

Fishing spiders sometimes fully submerge, and studies have shown that their eyesight remains reasonably good underwater. Their bodies have a "cuticle," or outer covering of a waxy, water-repelling substance that, combined with dense hair, keeps them dry. Only one species of spider lives in water, the "diving bell spider," or European water spider (*Argyroneta aquatica*; family Dictynidae). It spins a web among underwater plants and brings air down in its fine hairs to form a bubble, where it spends much of its life. The European water spider is not found in North America; it is a Palearctic species, primarily living in western Europe.

The genus name *Dolomedes* is combined from the Greek words δολος (dolos, "trick, stratagem") and μηδος (medos, "thought, intention"), according to Cameron. So maybe the fishing spider is the spider of wily plans.

A jumping spider.

JUMPING SPIDERS

Family Salticidae

Jumping spiders are wandering hunters, distinguishable by their two large front-facing eyes, which provide exceptionally keen vision, and usually squat bodies. They're daytime stalkers, also using ambush and wandering hunting techniques, who can turn up practically anywhere, from the wall or screens of your house, to brush, trees, and leaf litter, to sandy and stony shorelines. They don't spin snares, although like many hunting spiders they make silk retreats and egg sacs, as well as draglines that they fix to the ground to keep themselves oriented to their whereabouts.

They really do jump when pursuing prey or escaping predators. They fix an orienting dragline to the ground, get a running start, and launch anywhere from an inch or 2 to up to 25 times their own body length. Some have been seen leaping from vertical surfaces to ambush flying insects. Some use a kind of sit-and-wait strategy in which they keep still and use their extraordinary eyesight to watch for prey, then pursue it. Some jumping spiders invade the webs of other spiders and either steal prey that's already been snagged (a practice called kleptoparasitism) or attack and eat the owner of the web (called araneophagy). An Australian species, *Portia fimbriata*, uses a fascinating super-slow, robot-like

A jumping spider.

motion to stalk other jumping spiders. There are species of ant-like, wasp-like, and beetle-like mimics among the salticids.

Jumping spiders' marked distinction is that, along with a few species of wolf spiders, they have the best eyesight of any hunting spiders, whose vision is mainly far better than web spinners that detect prey by vibrations in silk rather than by sight. Jumping spiders have almost human-like image resolution within a range of a few inches, and when their cute-looking faces with their two huge (anterior median) goggle eyes are turned toward you, they appear to be curiously watching you—and may well be. Because of this, they are among the most painstakingly studied spiders. Researchers have found that jumping spiders can recognize images in pictures, respond to their own images in mirrors, and react to videos of other spiders as if the movie were real.

While many spiders court mainly by touch, vibrations (of silk), and scent (through pheromones), jumping spiders' keen eyesight also allows them to incorporate complex visual elements in their courtship displays. In many salticid species, the males use their striking colors in mating dances that involve different choreographies of leg and palp waving and body motions. In *Habronattus* genus jumpers, several species of which are found in Maine, the males' dance is accompanied by what amounts to singing, with distinctly rhythmic snaps of the legs and vibrations of the abdomen producing sound waves that the females

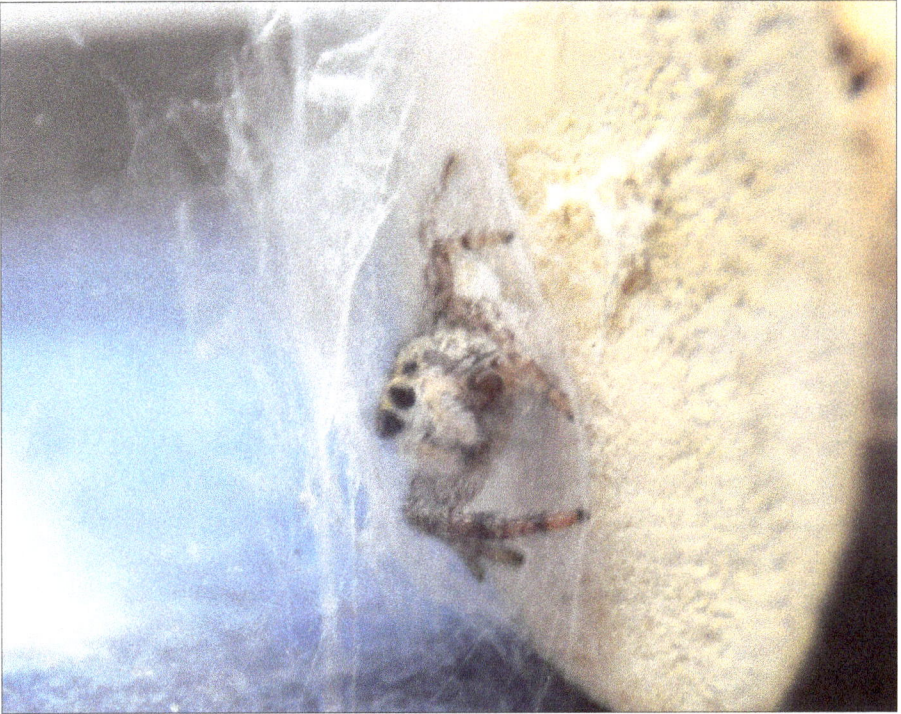

This jumping spider constructed a silk shelter within an hour of being captured.

somehow detect. The same male might use a primarily vibratory display to court a female in a nest, but use a primarily visual display for a female outside her nest. Salticid males have been observed courting immature females using vibratory displays; when he is accepted, he then builds a second silk chamber where he cohabits alongside her while he waits for her to mature—a not unusual practice among many spiders.

Jumping spiders tend to be stenochronous species, meaning they reproduce in spring or summer and overwinter as subadults. Many salticid females guard their egg sacs and recently hatched spiderlings. (In one species of salticid, *Toxeus magnus*, aka the black ant mimicking jumper, found in Southeast Asia, the mother feeds her young a milklike secretion for several weeks after they hatch.) Immature jumping spiders are generally inactive in winter and tend to enter diapause, or hibernate, in silk chambers, often spinning nests under bark in gatherings of the same or sometimes even other species.

Some jumping spiders are among the very few spiders whose jaws are strong enough to break human skin (others include some sac spiders, some wolf spiders, and some cobweb weavers). But with only a handful of exceptions in North America, a bite by almost all of these species is not dangerous and may not even be noticed unless you have an allergic reaction to the venom that in unusual cases can produce a typical itching, swelling, bug-bite type wound.

Jumping spiders make up the largest family of spiders worldwide, with more than 6,100 species identified in the *World Spider Catalog* in 2019. They were the third most abundant species collected in Jennings and Graham's Milbridge study.

The genus name *Salticus* is taken from the Latin adjective salticus, meaning "dancing"; the Latin words also carry connotations of jumping. The salticids are in a sense not just jumpers, but dancers.

Bronze jumper (*Eris militaris*)

The bronze jumper hunts in the open during the day, mainly in trees, shrubs, and tall grasses. The female is usually light brown, and the male is described as bronze-colored with white markings, and may appear darker. They overwinter as subadults and adults, and sometimes build hibernation retreats in large aggregations. The bronze jumper was the fourth most collected among all species in Jennings and Graham's Milbridge study.

The genus name *Eris* is from the Greek goddess of discord, strife, and war.

It's hard to tell for sure, but this spider appeared to be a bronze jumper (*Eris militaris*).

Two ground spiders copulating on a fence.

Communicating and Mating

Spiders have basically five ways of perceiving the physical world: visual, vibratory, acoustic, tactile, and chemical. Hunters, especially wolf spiders and jumping spiders, tend to have good vision for detecting prey. Web-weaving spiders' vision is generally less refined, as they read vibrations in silk and their surroundings to alert them to the presence of prey or predators.

In addition to possessing usually eight or six eyes, spiders have tiny organs on their bodies called slit sensilla, which detect different kinds of pressures in the spider's own body as well as in the environment, such as gravity and vibrations of air.

Slit sensilla on the spinnerets register movements of the silk spigots and dragline pressures, for example. Clusters of slit sensilla on the legs, called lyriform organs, detect air vibrations, or sound waves, meaning many spiders hear sounds—though whether spiders experience sound the same way humans do is of course unknown.

These different perceptual capabilities enable spiders to communicate with each other. One of the primary modes of communication is through vibrations of silk. For example, mated couples of the sheetweb weaver *Linyphia triangularis* may live together for several days in a web

123

A colorful male jumping spider (*Habronattus decorus*) in Fairfield, Maine. Photo by James Reben.

after mating, and they signal their individual identities to each other by vibrating the web to prevent mistaking the partner for prey. Similar signaling by silk vibrations occurs among the 20 or so species of social spiders (most of them species of theridiids, or cobweb weavers, and agelenids, or grass spiders), which live together in sometimes very large communities. Spiders' understanding of silk vibrations is so refined that some hunting spiders can imitate the vibrations of a struggling insect and trick a web owner into coming into range to be attacked. Ballooning spiders can tell

when wind and air conditions are right for flying.

Courtship and mating

These perceptual abilities come into play in spiders' courtship and mating rituals. Most adult male spiders prepare for the process by constructing a sperm web, a sheet or tube where they deposit the reproductive fluid in drops through an opening on their underside and then draw the fluid into their palps. They then go in search of a female.

Spiders with good vision, such as jumping spiders and wolf spiders, generally have strong visual components in their courtship. Males of many species of both families perform intricate dances for prospective mates, using precisely ritualized movements of palps, legs, and body. Among jumping spiders, males are often very colorful, and the colors are often displayed and concealed in different patterns during mating dances. Videos available on the internet show jumping spiders of the *Habronattus* genus (some species of which live in Maine) performing their astonishing dances.

Mating processes also involve other kinds of signals. A male may detect chemical signals, including pheromones, given off by the female herself or in her silk. Some spiders produce sounds during their mating dances by drumming or making clicking sounds with their legs, vibrating their abdomens, and making sounds with stridulatory, or scrape and file, organs that can be located, for example, on opposing parts of the abdomen and cephalothorax. Of course no one knows what a male or female spider's actual experience of these mating rituals is like, but visual and auditory mating displays are not random; they are as precisely made as orb webs. To put it in figurative terms, many male spiders sing and dance to attract a mate.

Courtship routines vary widely. Males of the *Tetragnatha* genus of long-jawed orbweavers simply seize the female's chelicerae with their fangs, without preliminaries, and proceed to the copulation position. Most male spiders approach a female cautiously, and may tap or vibrate dragline or web silk to attract her attention. A number of meanings could be communicated in this way, including signaling that the male is not a prey item. In some spiders, if the female does not attack, flee, or send rejection signals, the male delicately moves forward and gently taps or strokes the female.

One reason most males approach gingerly is that the female may attack and eat them; whether this is because the female mistakes the male for prey, or is just hungry, or is violently rejecting sex, or is acting according to an overall reproductive strategy of the species, is unclear. Among Palearctic nursery web spiders (*Pisaura mirabilis*), the male frequently offers a dead fly as a gift to a prospective mate.

The actual act of copulation involves the male mounting the female in one of about four general patterns, but each species has its own process whose descriptions could fill a Kama Sutra on spider sexual behavior. Some copulate in the web, some on the ground, some suspended on a thread of silk. Once in place on the female, the male uses his palps, one at a time, to insert sperm into the female's epigynum located underneath her abdomen. Again, different species follow different routines, but copulations have been observed to last anywhere from a few seconds to a few minutes, among, for example, a tropical species of jumping spider, *Plexippus paykulli*, and up to several hours among some species of wolf spider; copulations among one species of long-jawed orbweavers (*Tylorida ventralis*) in Indonesia were observed to go on almost continuously from dawn to dusk over several days.

Sometimes the female spider eats the male spider after, or even during copulation, but the frequency of sexual cannibalism, as it's called, varies widely from species to species. Overall, most spider mating does not result in the male's death. But sex is not safe for all spider males. Among some species of fishing spiders (*Dolomedes*), it appears that females eat males after copulation every time; nearly the same rate of death was observed for the orbweaver *Argiope bruennichi*, a European cousin of our banded garden spider (*Argiope trifasciata*). In experiments with cross spiders (*Araneus diadematus*), 40 percent of matings resulted in sexual cannibalism. Among black widow spiders (*Latrodectus*) in North America, the male generally escapes unscathed, but not always. The Australian redback male (*Latrodectus hasselti*) twists his abdomen directly over the female's fangs, and during the copulation she partially eats him;

he then pulls free, engages a second courtship, and repeats the maneuver, during which about two-thirds of redback males finally die. In a study of the sheetweb weaver *Neriene litigiosa* (found primarily in western North America), only one instance of sexual cannibalism was observed in 1,150 matings.

Males of some species die spontaneously during or shortly after copulation. Among nursery web spiders, males sometimes play dead during or after copulation (a strategy called thanatosis), often escaping being eaten. Males of cobweb weavers in the genus *Tidarren*, found in the Southeast, self-amputate one palp on the final molt, and use the remaining palp to accomplish mating; the *Tidarren argo* female tears that remaining palp off the male while they are copulating, and the dismembered member remains attached to the epigynum and functioning for several hours, as the female consumes the male. The advantage of this behavior is, so far, inexplicable.

In still other species, the male and female peacefully cohabit the web for a period of time after mating. Some species of widow spiders (*Latrodectus*) live together for weeks and share food. Cellar spiders (*Pholcus*) similarly live together in adjacent webs, and the male, who uncharacteristically for spiders is the dominant partner, brings food to the female. ✳

Hentzia mitrata

Hentzia mitrata is also known informally as the white-jawed jumping spider because the males, which are usually reddish in color with white stripes down the sides, have a white mustache of hairs that sometimes appears quite bushy. The females are usually light gray with subtle brown markings. They tend to hunt on plants. The male pictured here was patrolling our living room ceiling. Jumping spiders are known to sip plant nectar, and *H. mitrata* has been observed doing so.

The white-jawed jumping spiders' courtship ritual is less intricate than many other species of Salticidae. Observations indicate the females tend to resist males' advances, which consist of running fast toward the female as soon as he locates her, touching her with his front legs, and then immediately attempting to mount her. The females often run away and, if the male succeeds in mounting her, will disengage within a few seconds, whereupon the male gives chase. One researcher saw a male successfully pursue and mount a female five times.

White-jawed jumping spiders overwinter as subadults.

Hentzia mitrata has been identified in Maine, Québec, and New England; none turned up in Jennings and Graham's Milbridge study.

The genus name *Hentzia* was coined to honor Nicholas Marcellus Hentz, the "father of American arachnology" in the 19th century; *mitrata* is Latin for wearing a mitre, the tall headdress worn by bishops of the church.

This white-jawed jumping spider (*Hentzia mitrata*) was walking along the living room ceiling.

Dimorphic jumper (*Maevia inclemens*)

The dimorphic jumper is an interesting spider because there are two distinctly different morphs of the male, both of which differ distinctly from the female. The female is much larger than the males and is pale to tan colored with two reddish lines on her abdomen. Meanwhile, one of the male forms is black with striking tufts of hair on its head, and the other male form is gray with orange markings on its abdomen.

The two morphs have distinctly different courtship rituals. The tufted form attracts females starting from a distance of about 9 cm (3½ inches) from her, stilting up on his legs and holding up and waving his two front legs. The gray male starts about 3 cm (just more than an inch) from the female and sidles back and forth. Studies showed that females had no particular preference for one morph over the other. Variations in female acceptance did correlate to the distances at which courtship began, with the tufted males more successful at a distance, and the gray males more successful nearer-by. The researchers concluded that whoever got the female's attention first usually succeeded.

No individuals of the dimorphic jumper were collected in Jennings and Graham's Milbridge study, but the earlier unpublished version of Jennings and Donahue's checklist of Maine spiders indicates several hundred documented in Maine. These spiders overwinter as juveniles and sometimes as adults.

Above: A female dimorphic jumper (*Maevia inclemens*) in Fairfield, Maine. Photo by James Reben.

Left: A male dimorphic jumper, tufted morph.

Naphrys pulex

Naphrys pulex is fairly common in our region, a relatively drably marked jumping spider, females brown with off-white, chevron-like patches, and males dark gray. It frequently shows up on the side of our house in central Maine, and can be found in hardwood leaf litter in dry woodlands, as well as bark, rock outcrops, and buildings. *Naphrys pulex* is known to prey on ants. Males mature in the winter and live well into fall; females are found from early spring to October. No individuals of *Naphrys pulex* were documented in the Milbridge study, which does indicate its presence, though, in nearby Jonesboro.

The genus name *Naphrys* is a contraction of "North American Euophrys," devised by the arachnologist G.B. Edwards in 2002 for a reclassification of several jumping spiders from the *Euophrys* genus.

Naphrys pulex.

Pelegrina proterva

Pelegrina proterva is a fairly small jumping spider that can be found hunting in deciduous trees and grasses as well as leaf litter. It is widespread in North America, particularly in the Northeast and eastern Canada. Individuals of *P. proterva* were found from May to October in the Milbridge study; they are thought to have a single-year life cycle.

Pelegrina proterva is nicknamed reckless jumper in some guidebooks and websites, but this is not an accepted name among arachnologists. The mid-20th century Spanish naturalist Pelegrin Franganillo Balboa named the *Pelegrina* genus after himself, an unusual move; *proterva* is a form of a Latin word meaning "arrogant" or "violent," and in some lexicons "reckless."

Pelegrina proterva.

Zebra jumper (*Salticus scenicus*)

Most of the zebra jumpers identified in Jennings and Graham's Milbridge study were found around human-built structures, including in a wood bin, on the floor of a house, and on a screen door, among other places. They have a reputation as a curious spider that seems to investigate anything that moves, including humans. Like the vast majority of spiders, zebra jumpers don't bite people. They can be found active during the day on tree trunks and rocks and among debris, in addition to human structures. *Salticus scenicus* is not native to Maine, and is a Eurasian (Palearctic) species that has traveled widely to other continents, such as North America, where it is present as far south as North Carolina and as far north as southern Canada. They overwinter as juveniles, and adults are found from spring through fall.

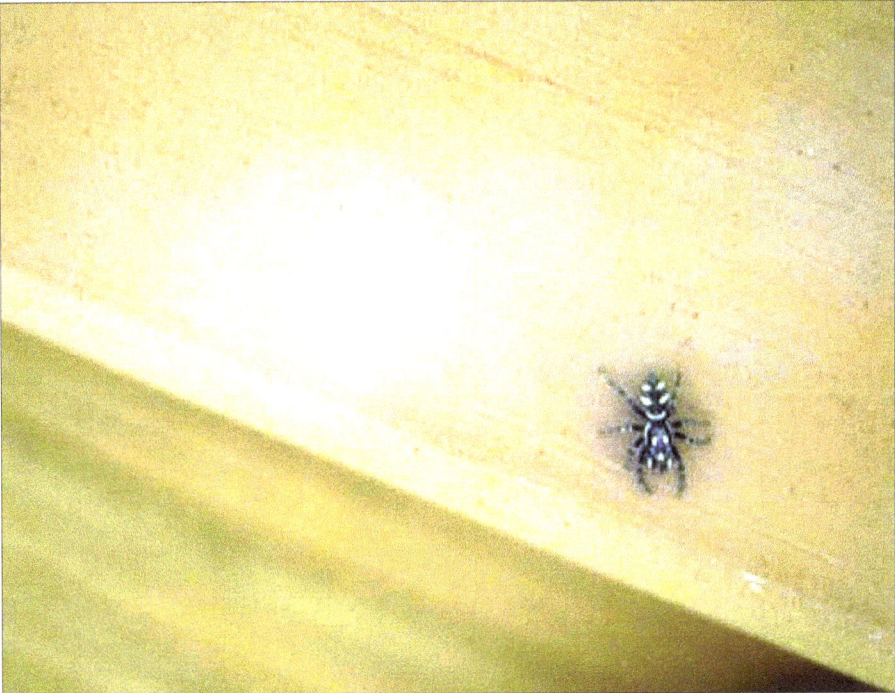

A zebra jumper (*Salticus scenicus*).

Sitticus fasciger

Sitticus fasciger is a small to medium-sized, brown jumping spider that is very comfortable around humans and is seen in and around buildings as often as anywhere else. A study of *S. fasciger* in Japan showed they have a two-year life cycle, overwintering as juveniles like most salticids. Because of this synanthropic disposition, the Japanese researchers thought it was likely *S. fasciger* was introduced into North America from Asia.

Three species of *Sitticus* genus jumpers turned up in Jennings and Graham's Milbridge study: *Sitticus floricola palustris*, *S. pubescens*, and *S. striatus*; the earlier unpublished version of Jennings and Donahue's checklist of Maine spiders showed eight species, including *S. fasciger*.

A male *Sitticus fasciger* on a kitchen window screen..

A crab spider in late October sunlight.

CRAB SPIDERS
Family Thomisidae

Crab spiders get their common name from the fact that they look and to some extent even move like ocean crabs. They hold their legs so the front surface is on top (a laterigrade position), making a bowlike appearance, and the front two pairs of legs, which have spines that help them grasp prey, are often thicker-looking and more powerful than the rear two pairs. Crab spiders can also move forward, backward, and laterally with more dexterity than most spiders. They're distinguished from running crab spiders (family Philodromidae) by their differing eye patterns and by the running crab spiders' quicker movements and longer, more slender second pair of legs; both families' abdomens tend to be flat, but crab spiders are usually somewhat rounder and tend to be more colorfully marked than running crab spiders.

Crab spiders are mainly sit-and-wait or stalking hunters who spin no webs for snares, retreats, or molting nests, though they still make silk for draglines and egg sacs. There are, generally speaking, two categories of crab spiders: those found usually on flowers, and those found usually on the ground, bark, or vegetation. They have keen eyesight at short distances, and readily detect prey movement up to 20 cm (about 8 inches) away. They stalk or ambush insects, grab them with the strong, spined front legs, and then bite them, making two tiny holes in the bug through which they suck out the innards. Some crab spiders also sip plant nectars as part of their diets.

Some crab spiders, such as those of the *Xysticus* and *Ozyptila* genera, which tend to be found on the ground or in vegetation, are winter-active, meaning they live and feed through the winter, mainly underneath the snow. Others, such as flower-dwellers like the goldenrod crab spider (*Misumena vatia*), tend to be winter-inactive, laying eggs that hatch in the fall, with the spiderlings overwintering in the sac.

Crab spiders are among the most widely distributed spider families, with more than 2,100 species identified worldwide in the *World Spider Catalog* in 2019. They were the seventh most abundant family collected in Jennings and Graham's Milbridge study.

Cameron indicates the French naturalist Charles Walckenaer in the 18th to 19th centuries invented the genus name *Thomisus* from the rare ancient Greek word θωμισσω (thomisso), meaning "whip, scourge, tie, bind," apparently connecting it to his observation that the crab spiders in question "spy out their prey stretching out a single thread of silk to catch it."

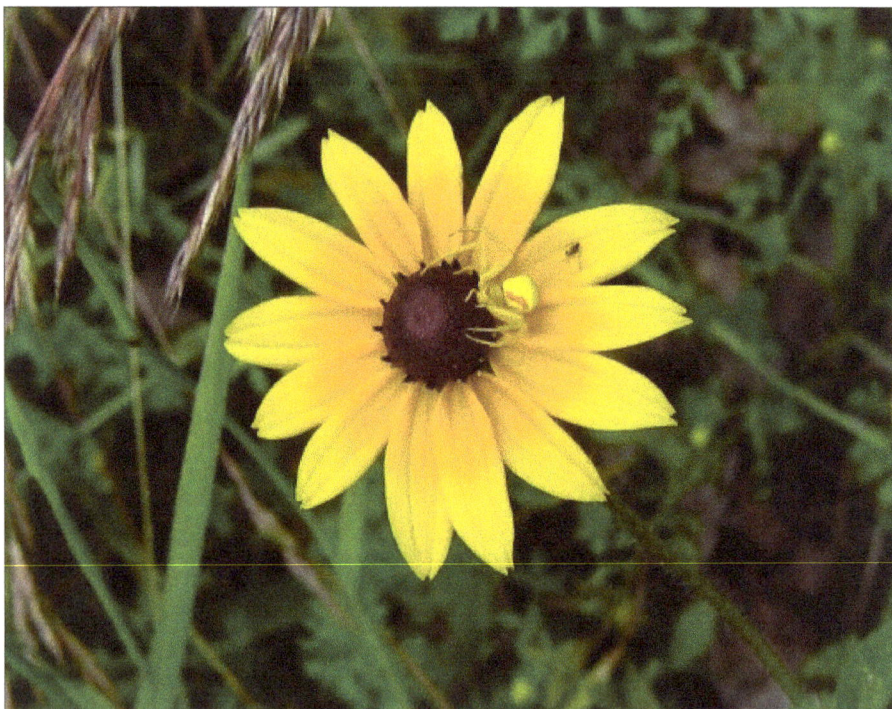

A goldenrod crab spider (*Misumena vatia*) waits on a black-eyed susan in Burnham, Maine.

A goldenrod crab spider capturing a bee.

A crab spider.

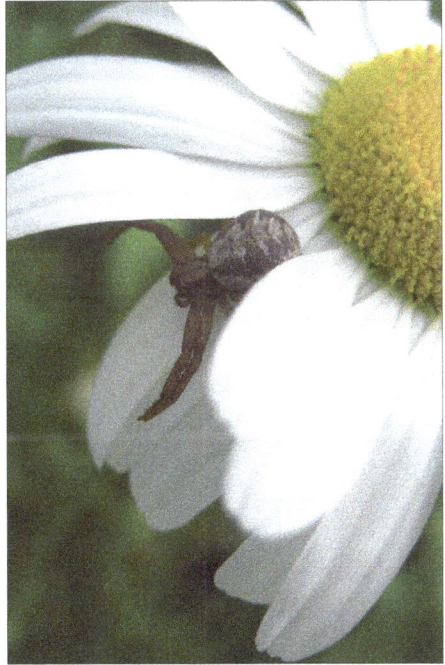

A tan crab spider (*Xysticus ferox*).

Bark crab spiders (*Bassaniana*)

Bark crab spiders closely resemble ground crab spiders (*Xysticus*), but have a flatter carapace and are sometimes darker colored to help them blend in with their common habitats, which include the bark of trees, fences, and wooden buildings. Occasionally they're found inside houses, too; the female shown in the photo was patrolling the top of the washing machine in our basement.

Bassaniana utahensis has been fairly commonly identified in Maine, along with morphs of *B. versicolor*, according to the earlier unpublished version of Jennings and Donahue's checklist, and it turned up in some numbers in Jennings and Graham's Milbridge study.

Jennings and Graham refer to this spider as *Coriarachne utahensis*, an earlier designation; the official *World Spider Catalog* name is *Bassaniana utahensis*. The genus name *Bassaniana* is a late 19th century tweak to *Bassania*, which was first used in moth and butterfly taxonomies. It's not known exactly where the word *Bassania* came from, though it was the ancient Latin name of the town of Elbasan in Albania. *Coriarachne* is invented from Greek words that translate, roughly, to "a spider that looks like a bedbug," according to Cameron, and was coined originally to distinguish these spiders from *Xysticus*.

A bark crab spider (*Bassaniana utahensis*) captured in a vial.

Goldenrod crab spider (*Misumena vatia*)

The goldenrod crab spider is often seen sitting on flowers waiting for prey. It's typically white or yellow, may have streaks of orange, red, or pink, and can change color to some extent to match its surroundings and make it less noticeable to potential prey. It closely resembles the whitebanded crab spider, but can be distinguished by the lack of a white ridge under its eyes. Goldenrod crab spiders are well known for attacking honeybees, which they grab by the head then eat while holding it in their jaws. Their eggs hatch in the summer or fall, and the spiderlings overwinter inside the sac.

The genus name *Misumena* is from the Greek μισουμένη (misoumeini, "(she) being hated"), according to Cameron. Its 18th century scientific name was *Araneus vatius*, "bow-legged spider."

Above: A goldenrod crab spider (*Misumena vatia*) eating a bee.

Left: A goldenrod crab spider on a wild rose petal.

137

Whitebanded crab spider (*Misumenoides formosipes*)

The whitebanded crab spider, also known in some guidebooks as the red-band-ed crab spider or the ridge-faced flower spider, resembles the goldenrod crab spider but has the white ridge under the eyes. This spider is usually white but can vary in color, which it also changes in accord with its surroundings as it waits for prey on flowers. It bites its prey on the back of the neck rather than the head, as practiced by the goldenrod crab spider.

Adult male whitebanded crab spiders don't do much hunting, and instead spend their time searching for and guarding prospective mates. The females make an egg sac and lay eggs in September or October; the spiderlings overwinter in the egg sac.

No whitebanded crab spiders were collected in Jennings and Graham's Milbridge study, but they note that *Misumenoides* has been collected at Mount Desert Island. I've seen individuals crawling around my cars.

The genus name *Misuminoides* is derived from *Misumena* (see goldenrod crab spider) with the addition of a Greek suffix, -οειδηζ, (-oides, "having the form of"), according to Cameron.

A whitebanded crab spider (*Misumenoides formosipes*) on a cannabis leaf.

A whitebanded crab spider (*Misumenoides formosipes*) on a steering wheel.

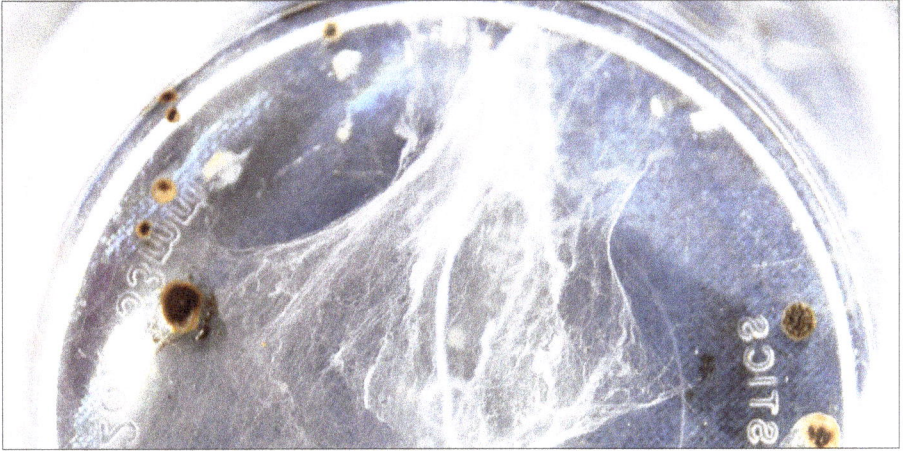

Droppings left in a vial by grass spiders and orbweavers.

Cleanliness is Next to Spiderliness

S ome spiders, it turns out, go out of their way to keep their surroundings clean.

Most spiders eat by capturing a prey item, such as a fly, disabling it with venom, then washing it with digestive juices and sucking the liquid through their mouths with the stomach, which acts like a pump. Many orbweavers perform a kind of chewing or shredding of body parts in the process of getting the pre-digested meat material into their mouths, and some have been seen using their palps to clean their mouth parts afterward. The liquid and pre-chewed material gets processed in the stomach, located in the spider's cephalothorax, and the remains run through an intestine into the midgut located in the abdomen. Waste material from the midgut travels through tiny channels called Malpighian tubules to a cloaca, which holds the excrement until it can be discharged through the spider's anus.

Like many other creatures, when you take a close look, spiders do not defecate randomly. In a study of adult female goldenrod crab spiders (*Misumena vatia*) living on milkweed and wild marjoram plants in South Bristol, Maine, a researcher found that the spiders had a common routine of scurrying to the tip of a petal or leaf, lifting themselves on their large front legs, with their abdomens raised, and releasing drops of a whitish liquid which fell either all the way to the ground or onto a lower leaf of, for example, a milkweed plant. Captured goldenrod crab spiders, when allowed to climb to the rim of a vial, did the same thing, making sure the waste material cleared the rim.

Another study in Missouri on black-and-yellow garden spiders (*Argiope aurantia*), which are fairly large spiders that are often seen in their orb webs hereabouts, similarly followed particular routines for going to the bathroom, like we say. These spiders tend to hang upside down at the center of their webs for long stretches of time. So if they were to defecate at random with the anus pointing up, the excretions would fall down and foul themselves and the webs. The researchers found the spiders had two methods of solving this, usually at night.

One was to shift around on the web so the anus pointed down, or nearly so, and let the dropping fall clear of the silk. In the second method, the spider attached a line of silk to the hub of the web and used it to descend to about the level of the bottom of the web. The spider then turned its body so the anus pointed straight down, released a dropping, then climbed back up the line of silk (or dropline, no pun). The whole process usually took 10 to 15 seconds.

The spiders' cleanliness might be a way of avoiding predators. In other words, if a wasp spots evidence of prey on the ground, it might look

Spider droppings in a vial.

around futilely on the ground, instead of up on the milkweed plant or in the web. Another motive for cleanliness might be to avoid driving away potential prey: the presence of excretions might alert bugs to the spider's presence and drive them away from the web or the hunting vicinity of the crab spider.

Goldenrod crab spiders who were held in vials routinely waited until they were released to defecate, even up to 47 days later. They just do not want to foul their immediate surroundings, it seems. ✳

Tmarus angulatus

Sometimes called the angled crab spider, *Tmarus angulatus* is a relatively small crab spider that stalks prey on shrub and tree leaves. It's usually brown or mottled-appearing, and has a particularly high clypeus, or space between the chelicerae and eyes. Its abdomen is higher than its head and rises toward the back to a small protrusion, or tubercle, which may vary in size from individual to individual. The spider shown here was found resting on a marijuana plant growing outside on the deck, with her long front legs positioned straight out in front of her.

Female *T. angulatus* spiders build a retreat, lay their eggs inside, and stand guard until they hatch. The spiderlings overwinter in their subadult instar and mature in spring.

Jennings and Graham found a few *T. angulatus* specimens in woods and on man-made structures during their Milbridge survey, and the earlier unpublished version of Jennings and Donahue's checklist of Maine spiders showed several dozen identified statewide.

Cameron indicates *Tmarus* was the ancient name of present-day Mount Tomaros in Greece. The French naturalist Eugène Simon, of the 19th and early 20th centuries, grabbed the name expediently from a dictionary.

Tmarus angulatus.

Ground crab spiders (*Xysticus*)

Ground crab spiders tend to be gray, tan, brown, or reddish brown, in contrast to the colors of the goldenrod and whitebanded crab spiders. They make their living mainly hunting on the ground, but some, such as *Xysticus ferox* and the elegant crab spider (*X. elegans*), are found in low vegetation and occasionally around flowers. The elegant crab spider, which one guidebook says might be the spider most commonly seen in the eastern U.S., is known to ambush prey much larger than itself, such as moths. A study in Manitoba found elegant crab spiders and *X. emertoni* to be winter-active under snow.

Crab spiders tend to have minimalist mating rituals in comparison to the elaborate rituals of some other spiders, such as jumping spiders. But in the *Xysticus* courtship ritual, the male ties the female to the ground with lines of silk, and then crawls underneath her to copulate. It's not certain what the advantage of this routine is, because the silk is not tight enough to serve as protection for the male—the female easily slips out of the bonds when mating is completed.

An elegant crab spider (*Xysticus elegans*).

A tan crab spider (*Xysticus ferox*).

Half of the roughly 130 species of crab spiders found north of Mexico belong to the *Xysticus* genus. More than a dozen species of *Xysticus* are found in Maine, including 10 species in Jennings and Graham's Milbridge study.

According to Cameron, the genus name *Xysticus* comes from a Latin cognate of the Greek word ξυστικοσ, meaning "pertaining to an athlete"; the word is related to the Greek verb ξυω (xeo, "to scrape") in association with ancient athletes' practice of cleaning themselves by rubbing their bodies with olive oil and then scraping the coating off.

Endangered Spiders

Spiders, like every other creature on Earth, face difficulties as global climate change affects ecosystems. But overall, spiders are well-positioned to keep pace, mainly because most are generalists. Since their food sources are diversified, a catastrophic reduction in one or even several arthropod populations in a given area will tend to have only small ramifications for spiders. For example, extensive flooding in an area can all but wipe out some species of invertebrates normally eaten by spiders, but it can also lead to a population boom among crickets, which thrive in post-flood terrain; instead of suffering from the sudden absence of some usual food sources, spiders in a flood-ravaged area can (theoretically) feast on the crickets.

Spiders are not immune to the disruptions of climate change, though. A study of spiders in Greenland published in 2018, for example, revealed that over 18 years, populations declined in several species of high arctic spiders "in response to rising temperatures and snow depth dynamics." The researchers reported that no spider species studied increased in abundance through the study period, 1996-2014.

The Endangered Species List maintained by the U.S. Fish & Wildlife Service includes eight species of spiders, six of which are in Texas and one in Hawaii, the Kaua'i cave wolf spider (*Adelocosa anops*). The eighth is the spruce-fir moss spider (*Microhexura montivaga*), a tiny tarantula, native to North Carolina and Tennessee; its high-altitude habitat is shrinking as balsam wooly adelgid true bugs are decimating fir forests and leading to dried-up moss, which the spiders need moist to survive.

As of mid-2019, no spider species appeared on Maine's lists of endangered or threatened species, and no spider species appeared on endangered lists of neighboring Nova Scotia, New Brunswick, Québec, New Hampshire, Massachusetts, Vermont, or New York state. In New England, only the black purse-web spider (*Sphodros niger*), a rarely found mygalomorph, is listed by Connecticut as a species of special concern. The black purse-web spider has not been found in Maine.

The International Union for Conservation of Nature's red list of endangered species, as compiled in 2019 from multiple agencies tracking endangered animals worldwide, included about 60 species of spiders, none of which is found in Maine. ✳

Spiders Uncommon or Rare in Maine

Animals don't recognize political borders, of course, and so spiders that are not established residents in the Maine area sometimes turn up. Following are brief descriptions of some of those spiders mentioned in Jennings and Graham's Milbridge study, in the early unpublished version of Jennings and Donahue's checklist of Maine spiders, and in a 2007 article by Daniel Jennings, Charlene Donahue, and Jonathan Mays for *The Maine Entomologist*.

Ninety-six percent of the spiders that occur in North America north of Mexico are araneomorphs, distinguished by the side-to-side arrangements of their jaws; all of the spiders that occur in Maine are araneomorphs. The other 4 percent of "true spiders" are mygalomorphs, whose jaws strike downward, horizontally. No mygalomorphs are known to be established in Maine, but tarantulas (family Theraphosidae) are sometimes brought here as pets. Another mygalomorph, the foldingdoor trapdoor spider (family Antrodiaetidae), which builds burrows with intricate doorway mechanisms, could be present in Maine because they've been identified in adjacent areas in Canada and New England.

Araneomorphs in the *Maine Entomologist* article's list of spiders that are "immigrants, i.e., species accidentally introduced, or invasive, or deliberately imported" into Maine but not established here include: wandering spiders (family Ctenidae), a primarily tropical family of hunters; woodlouse spiders (family Dysderidae), accidentally introduced from Europe to North America, with six eyes and huge chelicerae, preying on pill bugs; giant crab spiders, aka huntsman spiders (family Sparassidae, formerly Heteropodidae), very large spiders whose normal range is the Southwest and northern Mexico, one species of which reaches nearly 2 inches in body length; flatties (family Selenopidae), crab spiders with very flat bodies; and recluse spiders (family Sicariidae), including the brown recluse, whose bite can be medically significant, but whose range is the southern Midwest down to the Gulf of Mexico, and which has been captured as accidental imports to Maine only three times in recent years, according to entomologist Don Barry of the University of Maine Cooperative Extension.

Not mentioned in the *Maine Entomologist* article's list are the widow spiders (*Latrodectus* genus), which turn up accidentally from time to time in freight from states farther south. The bite of black widow and brown widow spiders can be medically significant, but "it's been something like 50 years or more since anyone in the U.S. died from a widow bite," Don Barry told me in 2015. "The last widow we caught in Maine, in the wild," he wrote, "was found in a rodent bait station behind the Walmart in Newport about five years ago—it was considered a hitchhiker. For myself, I've never seen one outdoors in Maine, and I think it's wrong to say that they are established in the state."

Araneomorphs that have not been seen in Maine but Jennings believes may be present because they're seen nearby in Canada or New England include: purseweb spiders (family Atypidae); goblin spiders (family Oonopidae); and prodidomids (family Prodidomidae), relatives of ground spiders (family Gnaphosidae).

Spiders of Milbridge and the earlier unpublished version of Jennings and Donahue's checklist of Maine spiders mention several families of spiders that have been identified but are not numerous in Maine. Those families include:

Ghost spiders (family Anyphaenidae), mostly small hunting spiders that stay in more or less constant motion during their active times as they scurry around vegetation; no ghost spiders were collected in the Milbridge study, but one species was identified elsewhere in Washington County, and Jennings and Donahue's unpublished checklist of Maine spiders indicates three species found in Maine.

Longlegged sac spiders (family Cheiracanthiidae (synonymous with Eutichuridae)), nocturnal hunters closely related to sac spiders (family Clubionidae) in behavior and, in some species, appearance; *Cheiracanthium mildei*, which the earlier unpublished version of Jennings and Donahue's checklist indicated had been identified seven times in Maine, may in unusual cases deliver a painful but not dangerous bite to humans; *Cheiracanthium mildei* and *Strotarchus piscatorius* mentioned in Jennings and Donahue's checklist were recently reclassified from family Miturgidae (prowling spiders); the Milbridge study mentions neither *Cheiracanthium*, *Strotarchus*, nor family Miturgidae.

Spinylegged sac spiders (family Liocranidae), hunting spiders found in moist low areas; unlike their cousins the sac spiders (family Clubionidae), they do not spin a retreat; they were the 16th most abundant family identified in the Milbridge study, out of 19 categories.

Pirate spiders (family Mimetidae, aka cannibal spiders), hunting spiders that prey largely on other spiders and their eggs, sometimes in sit-and-wait mode, sometimes approaching webs and drawing out the owner by plucking strands of the web; no pirate spiders were found in the Milbridge study but they are among the spiders Jennings and Graham say are likely present there, as species have been found in Cherryfield and Mount Desert Island; the earlier unpublished version of Jennings and Donahue's checklist of Maine spiders indicated four species in Maine.

Dwarf cobweb weavers (family Mysmenidae), tiny spiders that spin small, very unusual three-dimensional orb webs near the ground; they are a mostly tropical family, but the *Mysmena québecana* species has been found in Québec; the genus and species of one dwarf cobweb weaver found in Maine could not be determined by arachnologists, and the specimen is now housed in the arachnid collection at the Museum of Comparative Zoology at Harvard University.

Cave cobweb spiders (family Nesticidae), a small cave-dwelling spider similar to sheetweb weavers and cobweb weavers; identified just once in Maine, according to the earlier unpublished version of Jennings and Donahue's checklist of Maine spiders.

Flatmesh weavers (family Oecobiidae), a tiny spider that builds sheetwebs, often in human habitations, but has been found just once in Maine.

Lynx spiders (family Oxyopidae), hunting spiders with conspicuous spines on their legs, known as crafty stalkers; at least nine specimens of the western lynx spider (*Oxyopes scalaris*) have been found in Maine, as indicated in Jennings and Donahue's unpublished checklist of Maine spiders; not mentioned in the Milbridge study.

Spitting spiders (family Scytotidae), a six-eyed hunting spider, mainly tropical, that stalks its prey and then subdues it by spitting a mixture of venom and glue that tacks the bug to the substrate and poisons it; two specimens have been found in Maine, according to the earlier unpublished version of Jennings and Donahue's checklist of Maine spiders; not mentioned in the Milbridge study.

Ray orbweavers (family Theridiosomatidae), a small orbweaving spider that also hunts. *Theridiosoma gemmosum*, found only rarely in Maine, spins an orb web that the spider pulls into a cone shape, then sits and waits on a nearby silk platform; when a bug strikes the web, the ray orbweaver releases the tension and springs the snare, entangling the bug. Jennings and Graham list the ray orbweaver as a spider likely to be present in Milbridge, as it has been identified on Mount Desert Island.

Rock weavers (family Titanoecidae), a cribellate spider (producing messy-looking silk) resembling hackledmesh weavers (family Amaurobiidae), with which they were formerly classified; one adult female was collected in the Milbridge study, and the earlier unpublished version of Jennings and Donahue's checklist of Maine spiders indicated just three specimens found in Maine overall.

Hackled (or hackleband) orbweavers (family Uloboridae), a cribellate spider (producing messy-looking silk) that builds a horizontal orb web, and does not use venom to subdue prey; rarely found in Maine, the hackled orbweaver is mentioned by Jennings and Graham as a spider identified on Mount Desert Island, but not in the Milbridge study; two other species have been identified elsewhere in Maine, according to the earlier unpublished version of Jennings and Donahue's checklist of Maine spiders.

A jumping spider in East Sebago, Maine.

A cobweb weaver.

An orbweaver.

A filmy dome spider (sheetweb weaver).

A cellar spider.

A nursery web spider.

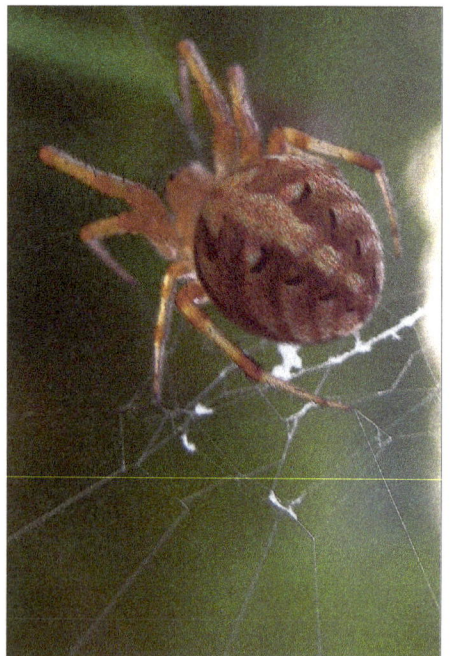

An arabesque orbweaver.

Humans in Monsters' Bodies

My fascination for spiders started years ago amid a general self-imposed awakening to the details of the woods. I was head-first in flower, tree, bird, and bug facts I had never taken time to really sort out because the feelings of awe always seemed more important than the mastery of names. But the names started to feel like a layer of the different kinds of awe—a flock of Canada geese reflects one facet of cosmic beauty, a pair of blister beetles on a rose petal another. These birds and bugs, I was thinking, have names that might be illuminating.

It turned out to be complicated. *Branta canadensis* is an object; a flock of geese rising over the lake in still evening air is something else.

Another thing was the population of black-and-yellow garden spiders that had set up their orb webs in the brush at the Unity park. If one noticed you getting too close, she started bouncing her web, as if she was stuck to a vertical trampoline. Maybe the bouncing web was a threat, or maybe a diversion, or a blurring tactic, who knows exactly what she thought she was doing.

Whatever else was happening, the spider was: 1. watching me and 2. thinking.

Now, to remain grounded in the real world of natural fact, you have to immediately realize that what the words "watching" and "thinking" refer to in a spider's experience can't possibly be the same as what they refer to in a human's experience. You can see that the garden spider is small, it lives in a web, it's constantly at risk of being attacked and swallowed by huge beings from above or below, and it visits its own shocking savagery on smaller beings yet. A spider takes completely different meaning from its surroundings than humans do. But it is, nonetheless, meaning.

Jumping spiders, I soon discovered, have much better eyesight than garden spiders. When you encounter them, they look right at you in ways the garden spiders can't. Dimorphic jumping spiders (*Maevia inclemens*), in a study, reacted to videos of prey and potential mates as if they were real. It's not known if a spider can recognize you personally, but in other studies, bees learned to distinguish between human faces. And jumping spiders watch you.

Spiders communicate with each other. For example, mated cellar spiders (family Pholcidae) send vibrations through web silk that are secret messages—"It's me, don't eat me!" Dewdrop spiders (*Neospintharus*) send vibrations that trick another spi-

A black-and-yellow garden spider (*Argiope aurantia*).

der into coming out of its own web so they can steal the catch or even attack and eat the owner. Spiders detect sound waves, too, and process them to extract information about their surroundings—meaning that in their own way, spiders hear.

You might think their brains are too small to be generating anything like what we call "meaning." But recent theories of mental capacities suggest that it's not the number of brain cells that matters in intelligence; rather, the proportion of the brain's physical size to the body's physical size is a better indicator of a being's relative intelligence. Crow brains are much smaller than chimpanzee brains, but studies indicate crows are every bit as clever as chimps. Some species of orchard spiders (*Leucage mariana*, found in Maine) and jumping spiders (*Phidippus clarus*, also found in Maine) have brains so big that they spill down into their body cavities and legs early in life, when they're still spiderlings.

What are the upper limits of a spider's sentience?

Some engineers in Great Britain taught regal jumping spiders (*Phidippus regius*) to leap between platforms so they could observe the mechanics of the spiders' leg motion; the training, interestingly, did not involve food bait. The spiders took a challenge and solved a problem. Somehow, the spiders think. Whatever that means.

Studies of a velvet spider (*Stegodyphus dumicola*) native to the Kalahari Desert in southern Africa showed that traits such as boldness, shyness, and task specialization within spider social structures varied from individual to individual in changing circumstances. Other studies on wolf spiders have made similar findings. Meaning that some spiders, at least, have individual personalities.

We can't get carried away with this and start speculating about spider philosophers meditating in the brush at the park—that's science fiction (see for example Adrian Tchaikovsky's novel *Children of Time*). But sentience has many more facets than only the ability to reason abstractly and then talk about it. Big brains, complex webs. Spiders are having experiences we can probably never understand, the same way we're having experiences they can never understand.

My wife, Bonnie, loves her backyard encounters with nature's cosmic beauty. She likes to drive the back road through nearby Thorndike to see the Canada geese drift on the still water of a pond there. Mysterious, they perennially are, beautiful. She's not interested in their scientific name. But they seem almost human to her. By what lake's edge or pool will they build after they fly away, she wonders, and what will that family's life be like?

"They're like the best part of people, and with wings," she says.

Spiders are a different story. Strange. Alien-looking. Threatening.

"But they're just making a living like us," I always say, "like the geese and everybody else. And the vast majority of them aren't the least bit dangerous to humans."

My words avail not much.

"They give me the creeps," she says.

"They're just humans in monsters' bodies," I say.

"Anyway, thank goodness they're small. Who knows what they'd be thinking about us." ✳

A black-and-yellow garden spider in Milbridge, Maine.

To a Garden Spider

Dangling over the zucchini like a dangerous jewel,
you set up housekeeping amid the gladioli,
your silken web spanning stiff green blades,
and you, poised in its eye, alert to possibilities,
a black face silhouetted in yellow horror.

Below, squash bugs swarm the zucchini
leaving fat leaves in ashen heaps. I pluck
one from the horde and drop it onto your web.
Its six black feet catch fast in the interstices.
Your reaction is unequivocal.

A ripple of legs carries you to your victim.
You cradle it in your eight-fold embrace.
A swaddling in shrouds from your spinnerets,
one paralyzing kiss, then you leave your prey
dangling to retake your silent center.

Your web is eloquent—a Charlotte's web.
You write words with your artistry.
And what lessons, I wonder, would you teach me
about solitude and survival? What could I learn
from your deadly attention to detail?

by Leslie Moore

List of Works Consulted

Aitchison, C.W. "Low temperature feeding by winter-active spiders." *Journal of Arachnology* Vol. 12, 1984.

—. "The phenology of winter-active spiders." *Journal of Arachnology* Vol. 12, 1984.

Aitchison, Cassie. "Feeding ecology of winter-active spiders" in *Ecophysiology of Spiders*, Wolfgang Nentwig, ed. Springer, 1987.

Albo, Maria J. "Sexual selection, ecology and evolution of nuptial gifts in spiders" via ResearchGate, 2017.

Albo, Maria J., and Alfredo V. Peretti. "Worthless and nutritive nuptial gifts: mating duration, sperm stored and potential female decisions in spiders." *Plos One*, June 2015.

Albo, Maria J., Søren Toft, and Trine Bilde. "Female spiders ignore condition-dependent information from nuptial gift wrapping when choosing mates." *Animal Behaviour* Vol. 84, 2012.

Albo, Maria J., Gudrun Winther, Cristina Tuni, Søren Toft, and Trine Bilde. "Worthless donations: male deception and female counter play in a nuptial gift-giving spider." *BMC Evolutionary Biology* Vol. 11, 2011.

Andrade, Maydianne C.B., and Erin M. Banta. "Value of male remating and functional sterility in redback spiders." *Animal Behaviour* Vol. 63, 2002.

Arnqvist, Goran. "Courtship behavior and sexual cannibalism in the semi-aquatic fishing spider *Dolomedes fimbriatus* (Clerck) (Araneae: Pisauridae)." *Journal of Arachnology* Vol. 20, 1992.

Arnqvist, Goran, and Stefan Henriksson. "Sexual cannibalism in the fishing spider and a model for the evolution of sexual cannibalism based on genetic constraints." *Evolutionary Ecology* Vol. 11, 1997.

Atkins, James A., Curtis W. Wingo, and William A. Sodeman. "Probable cause of necrotic spider bite in the midwest." *Science* Vol. 126, 12 July 1957.

Baird, Craig R., and Robert L. Stoltz. "Range expansion of the hobo spider, *Tegenaria agrestis*, in the northwestern United States (Araneae, Agelenidae)." *Journal of Arachnology* Vol. 30, 2002.

Barnhart, Robert K., ed. *Chambers Dictionary of Etymology*. H.W. Wilson Co., 2006.

Barry, Donald. University of Maine Cooperative Extension. Personal communications, 2013-2016.

Barth, Friedrich G. *A Spider's World: Senses and Behavior.* Springer-Verlag Berlin Heidelberg New York, 2002.

Bascom, Nick. "The origin of orbs." *Science News,* Nov. 3, 2011.

Becker, Elizabeth, Susan Riechert, and Fred Singer. "Male induction of female quiescence/catalepsis during courtship in the spider *Agelenopsis aperta.*" *Behaviour* Vol. 142, 2005.

Bilde, Trine, Cristina Tuni, Rehab Elsayed, Stano Pekar, and Søren Toft. "Death feigning in the face of sexual cannibalism." *Biological Letters*, Vol. 2, 2006.

Blackledge, Todd A. "Spider silk: a brief review and prospectus on research linking biomechanics and ecology in draglines and orb webs." *Journal of Arachnology* Vol. 40, 2012.

Bond, Alan B. "The evolution of color polymorphism: crypticity, searching images, and apostatic selection." *Annual Review of Ecology, Evolution, and Systematics*, Vol. 38, 2007.

Bond, Jason E. "Seta-spigot homology and silk production in first instar *Antrodiaetus unicolor* spiderlings (Araneae: Antrodiaetidae)." *Journal of Arachnology* Vol. 22, 1994.

Bowden, J.J., and C.M. Buddle. "Egg sac parasitism of Arctic wolf spiders (Araneae: Lycosidae) from northwestern North America." *Journal of Arachnology* Vol. 40, 2012.

Bowden, Joseph J., Oskar Liset Pryds Hansen, Kent Olsen, and Niels Martin Schmidt. "Drivers of inter-annual variation and long-term change in High-Arctic spider species abundances." *Polar Biology*, June 2018.

Bradley, Richard A. *Common Spiders of North America.* University of California Press, 2013.

—. Personal communications, 2015-2016.

Breene, Robert Gale III. "Spider Digestion & Food Storage." www.atshq.org/articles/Digestion.pdf

Brierton, Bonnie M., Douglas C. Allen, and Daniel T. Jennings. "Spider fauna of sugar maple and white ash in northern and central New York state." *Journal of Arachnology* Vol. 31, 2003.

Bruce, J.A., and J.E. Carico. "Silk use during mating in *Pisaurina mira* (Walckenaer) (Araneae, Pisauridae). *Journal of Arachnology* Vol. 16, 1988.

Carico, James E. "The nearctic spider genus *Pisaurina* (Pisauridae)." *Psyche* Vol. 79, 1972.

Catley, Kefyn M. "Darwin's Missing Link—A Novel Paradigm for Evolution Education." Wiley InterScience, 27 April 2006.

—. Personal communications, 2017-2019.

—. "Supercooling and its ecological implications in *Coelotes atropos* (Araneae, Agelenidae)." *Journal of Arachnology* Vol. 20, 1992.

Chen, Zhanqi, Richard T. Corlett1, Xiaoguo Jiao, Sheng-Jie Liu, Tristan Charles-Dominique, Shichang Zhang, Huan Li, Ren Lai, Chengbo Long, and Rui-Chang Quan. "Prolonged milk provisioning in a jumping spider." *Science* Vol. 20, Nov. 30, 2018.

Clark, David L., and Carrie L. Morjan. "Attracting female attention: the evolution of dimorphic courtship displays in the jumping spider *Maevia inclemens* (Araneae: Salticidae)." *Proceedings of the Royal Society B*, Vol. 268, December 2001.

Collins, Judith A., Daniel T. Jennings, and H.Y. Forsythe, Jr. "Effects of cultural practices on the spider (Araneae) fauna of lowbush blueberry fields in Washington County, Maine." *Journal of Arachnology* Vol. 24, 1996.

Connecticut Department of Energy and Environmental Protection, *Connecticut's Endangered, Threatened and Special Concern Species 2015*.

Cramer, Kenneth L., and Alex V. Maywright. "Cold temperature tolerance and distribution of the brown recluse spider *Loxosceles reclusa* (Araneae, Sicariidae) in Illinois." *Journal of Arachnology* Vol. 36, 2008.

Crawford, Rod. "Myth: Spiders only 'suck juices' of prey." Burke Museum of Natural History and Culture website. www.burkemuseum.org/blog/myth-spiders-only-suck-juices-prey

Curtis, J. Thomas, and James E. Carrel. "Defaecation behaviour of Argiope aurantia (Araneae: Araneidae)." Bulletin of the British Arachnological Society Vol. 11, 2000.

Cutler, Bruce. "A new subspecies of *Philodromus rufus* (Araneae: Philodromidae)." *Journal of Arachnology* Vol. 31, 2003.

Dacke, Marie, Thuy A. Doan, and David C. O'Carroll. "Polarized light detection in spiders." *Journal of Experimental Biology* Vol. 204, 2001.

Dondale, Charles D., and James H. Redner. *The Insects and Arachnids of Canada Part 17: The Wolf Spiders, Nurseryweb Spiders, and Lynx Spiders of Canada and Alaska*. Agriculture Canada Publication 1856, 1990.

Dunlop, Jason A., David Penney, and Denise Jekel. "A summary list of fossil spiders and their relatives." *World Spider Catalog* online at http://wsc.nmbe.

ch, version 18.5, accessed 28 January 2018.

Eberhard, William G. "Araneus expletus (Araneae: Araneidae): another stabilimentum that does not function to attract prey." *Journal of Arachnology* Vol. 36, 2008.

—. "Under the influence: webs and building behavior of *Plesiometa argyra* (Araneae: Tetragnathidae) when parasitized by *Hymenoepimecis argyraphaga* (Hymenoptera: Ichneumonidae). *Journal of Arachnology* Vol. 29, 2001.

Edwards, G.B. "A review of the nearctic jumping spiders (Araneae: Salticidae) of the subfamily Euophryinae north of Mexico." *Insecta Mundi*, Vol. 16, 2002.

Elgar, Mark A. "Sexual cannibalism in spiders and other invertebrates" in *Cannibalism: Ecology and Evolution among Diverse Taxa*. Oxford University Press, 1992.

Elias, Damian O., Norman Lee, Eileen A. Hebets, and Andrew C. Mason. "Seismic signal production in a wolf spider: parallel versus serial multi-component signals." *Journal of Experimental Biology* Vol. 209, 2006.

Elias, Damian O., Andrew C. Mason, Wayne P. Maddison, and Ronald R. Ho. "Seismic signals in a courting male jumping spider (Araneae: Salticidae)." *Journal of Experimental Biology* Vol. 206, 2003.

Evans, Arthur V. *National Wildlife Federation Field Guide to Insects and Spiders.* Chanticleer Press Inc., 2007.

Fernandez, Rosa, Robert J. Kallal, Dimitar Dimitrov, Jesus A. Ballesteros, Miquel A. Arnedo, Gonzalo Giribet, and Gustavo Hormiga. "Phylogenomics, diversification dynamics, and comparative transcriptomics across the spider tree of life." *Current Biology* Vol. 28, 2018.

Figart, Frances. "The Benefits of Spiders—An Interview with Kefyn Catley." Great Smoky Mountains Association website, June 2018. www.smokiesinformation.org/news/the-benefits-of-spiders-an-interview-with-kefyn-catley

Foelix, Rainer F. *Biology of Spiders.* Oxford University Press, 2011.

Francis, David A., and Robert M. Leavitt. *Passamaquoddy-Maliseet Dictionary.* University of Maine Press, 2008.

Ghislandi, Paolo, Trine Bilde, and Cristina Tuni. "Extreme male mating behaviours: anecdotes in a nuptial gift-giving spider." *Arachnology* Vol. 16, 2005.

Gillung, Jéssica P., and Christopher J. Borkent. "Death comes on two wings: a review of dipteran natural enemies of arachnids." *Journal of Arachnology* Vol. 45, 2017.

Grinsted, Lena, and Jonathan P. Bacon. "Animal behaviour: task differentiation by personality in spider groups." *Current Biology* Vol. 24, 2014.

Graham, Frank, Jr. "Dan Jennings' Slice of Immortality." *The Maine Entomologist* Vol. 11, August 2007.

—. "Spiders Unmasked." *The Maine Entomologist* Vol. 15, August 2011.

—. "The Predator Plundered." Audubonmagazine.org April 29, 2009.

Greene, Albert, Jonathan A. Coddington, Nancy L. Breisch, Dana M. De Roche, and Benedict B. Pagac Jr. "An immense concentration of orb-weaving spiders with communal webbing in a man-made structural habitat (Arachnida: Araneae: Tetragnathidae, Araneidae)." *American Entomologist*, Fall 2010.

Hannum, Charles, Jr., and Dini M. Miller. "Widow spiders." Virginia Cooperative Extension. https://pubs.ext.vt.edu/444/444-422/444-422.html

Hansen, Line Spinner, Sofia Fernandez Gonzalez, Søren Toft, and Trine Bilde. "Thanatosis as an adaptive male mating strategy in the nuptial gift–giving spider *Pisaura mirabilis*." *Behavioral Ecology*, 2008.

Hathaway, William. *Dawn Chorus: New and Selected Poems* 1972-2017. Simondoco Press, 2018.

Heinrich, Bernd. *Summer World: A Season of Bounty*. Ecco, 2009.

Hentz, N.M. "A notice concerning the spiders whose web is used in medicine." *Journal of the Academy of Natural Sciences of Philadelphia*, Vol. 2, 1821.

Herberstein, M.E., C.L. Craig, J.A. Coddington, and M.A. Elgar. "The function significance of silk decorations of orb-web spiders: a critical review of the empirical evidence." *Biological Reviews of the Cambridge Philosophical Society*, Vol. 75, 2000.

Herberstein, M.E., A.E. Wignall, E.A. Hebets, and J.M. Schneider. "Dangerous mating systems: Signal complexity, signal content and neural capacity in spiders." *Neuroscience & Biobehavioral Reviews* Vol. 46, 2014.

Hill, D.E. "Notes on *Hentzia mitrata* (Hentz 1846) (Araneae: Salticidae: Dendryphantinae)." *Peckhamia* Vol. 91.1, June 2011.

Hillyard, Paul H. *The Book of the Spider*, Avon Books, 1998.

Houser, Jeremy D., Howard Ginsberg, and Elizabeth M. Jakob. "Competition between introduced and native spiders (Araneae: Linyphiidae)." *Biological Invasions* Vol. 16, 2014.

Houser, Jeremy D., Daniel T. Jennings, and Elizabeth M. Jakob. "Predation by *Argyrodes trigonum* on *Linyphia triangularis*, an invasive sheet-web weaver in coastal Maine." *Journal of Arachnology* Vol. 33, 2005.

Howell, W. Mike, and Ronald L. Jenkins. *Spiders of the Eastern United States: A Photographic Guide*, Pearson Education Inc., 2004.

Jackson, R.R., and F.R. Cross. "Spider cognition." *Advances in Insect Physiology* Vol. 41, 2011.

Jackson, Robert R., and Aynsley M. Macnab. "Display, mating, and predatory behaviour of the jumping spider *Plexippus paykulli* (Araneae: Salticidae)." *New Zealand Journal of Zoology* Vol. 16 1989.

Jakob, Elizabeth M., Adam H. Porter, Howard Ginsberg, Julie V. Bednarski, and Jeremy Houser. "A 4-year study of invasive and native spider populations in Maine." *Canadian Journal of Zoology* Vol. 89, 2011.

Jass, Joan P. *Life Cycle Patterns in Wisconsin Spiders.* Milwaukee Public Museum, 1995.

Japyassu, Hilton F., and Kevin N. Laland. "Extended spider cognition." *Animal Cognition* Vol. 20, 2017.

Jennings, Daniel T., Kefyn M. Catley, and Frank Graham, Jr. "*Linyphia triangularis*, a palearctic spider (Araneae: Linyphiidae) new to North America." *Journal of Arachnology* Vol. 30, 2002.

Jennings, D.T., and J.A. Collins. "Coniferous-habitat associations of spiders (Araneae) on red spruce foliage." *Journal of Arachnology* Vol. 14, 1987.

—. "Spiders on red spruce foliage in northern Maine." *Journal of Arachnology* Vol. 14, 1987.

Jennings, D.T., and J.B. Dimond. "Arboreal spiders (Araneae) on balsam fir and spruces in east-central Maine." *Journal of Arachnology* Vol. 16, 1988.

Jennings, Daniel T., and Charlene P. Donahue. "A preliminary checklist of Maine spiders (Arachnida: Araneae), including species found elsewhere in New England and in Atlantic Canada" (in preparation).

Jennings, Daniel T., Charlene Donahue, and Jonathan Mays. "Maine's Spider Fauna." *The Maine Entomologist* Vol. 11, May 2007.

Jennings, Daniel T., Charles D. Dondale, and James H. Redner. *An Annotated Checklist of the Spiders (Arachnida: Araneae) of Mount Katahdin, Baxter State Park, Maine, USA.* Maine Forest Service, 2012.

Jennings, Daniel T., and Frank Graham, Jr. *Spiders (Arachnida: Araneae) of Milbridge, Washington County, Maine.* 2007.

Jennings, D.T., and D.J. Hilburn. "Spiders (Araneae) captured in malaise traps in spruce-fir forests of west-central Maine." *Journal of Arachnology* Vol. 16, 1988.

Jennings, D.T., and M.W. Houseweart. "Sex-biased predation by web-spinning spiders (Araneae) on spruce budworm moths." *Journal of Arachnology* Vol. 17, 1989.

Jennings, D.T., M.W. Houseweart, C.D. Dondale, and J.H. Redner. "Spiders (Araneae) associated with strip-clearcut and dense spruce-fir forest of Maine." *Journal of Arachnology* Vol. 16, 1988.

Jennings, Daniel T., Jerry R. Longcore, and James E. Bird. "Spiders (Araneae) inhabit lepidopteran-feeding shelters on ferns in Maine, USA." *Journal of the Acadian Entomological Society* Vol. 13, 2017.

Jennings, Daniel T., and Ivan McDaniel. "*Latrodectus hesperus* (Araneae: Theridiidae) in Maine." *Entomological News* Vol. 99, January-February 1988.

Jennings, D.T., W.M. Vander Haegen, and A.M. Narahara. "A sampling of forest-floor spiders (Araneae) by expellant, Moosehorn National Wildlife Refuge, Maine." *Journal of Arachnology* Vol. 18, 1990.

Justice, Michael J., Teresa C. Justice, and Regina L. Vesci. "Web orientation, stabilimentum structure and predatory behavior of *Argiope florida* Chamberlin & Ivie 1944 (Araneae, Araneidae, Argiopinae)." *Journal of Arachnology* Vol. 33, 2005.

Kaston, B.J. *How to Know the Spiders.* William C. Brown Co., 1978.

—. "Is the black widow spider invading New England?" *Science* Vol. 119, 1954.

—. *Spiders of Connecticut.* State Geological and Natural History Survey of Connecticut, 1981.

Kaufman, Rachel. "Small spiders have big brains that spill into their legs." *National Geographic News*, November 2011.

Kim, Kil Won. "Variation in group cohesion during the maternal social period of a subsocial spider." *Entomological Research* Vol. 46, 2016.

Kim, Kil Won, Bertrand Krafft, and Jae Chun Choe. "Cooperative prey capture by young subsocial spiders." *Behavioral Ecology and Sociobiology* Vol. 59, 2005.

Kim, Kil Won, Chantal Roland, and Andre Horel. "Functional value of matriphagy in the spider *Amaurobius ferox*." *Ethology* Vol. 106, 1999.

Kiss, Balazs, and Ferenc Samu. "Comparison of autumn and winter development of two wolf spider species (*Pardosa*, Lycosidae, Araneae) having different life history patterns." *Journal of Arachnology* Vol. 30, 2002.

Lallo, Madeline, and George W. Uetz. "Good vibrations: Female response to signal components in *Schizocosa* ethospecies" (conference paper abstract). American Arachnological Society 42nd Annual Meeting, June 2018.

Langley, Ricky L. "Animal-related fatalities in the United States—an update." *Wilderness and Environmental Medicine* Vol. 16, 2005.

Levi, H.W. "The American orb-weaver genera *Dolichognatha* and *Tetragnatha* north of Mexico (Araneae: Araneidae, Tetragnathinae)." *Bulletin of the Museum of Comparative Zoology* Vol. 149, 1981.

Levi, Herbert W., and Lorna R. Levi. *Spiders and Their Kin.* St. Martin's Press, 2002.

Lewis, Sara M., Karim Vahed, Joris M. Koene, Leif Engqvist, Luc F. Bussiere, Jennifer C. Perry, Darryl Gwynne, and Gerlind U.C. Lehmann. "Emerging issues in the evolution of animal nuptial gifts." *Biology Letters* Vol. 10, 2014.

Mammola, Stefano, Peter Michalik, Eileen A. Hebets, and Marco Isaia. "Record breaking achievements by spiders and the scientists who study them." *PeerJ* Vol. 5, 2017.

Martyniuk, J., and D.H. Wise. "Stage-biased overwintering survival of the filmy dome spider (Araneae, Linyphiidae)." *Journal of Arachnology* Vol. 13, 1985.

McNett, Bonnie Jean, and Ann L. Rypstra. "Effects of prey supplementation on survival and web site tenacity of *Argiope trifasciata* (Araneae, Araneidae): a field experiment." *Journal of Arachnology* Vol. 25, 1997.

Miles, Judith S. NASA Web formation experiment (ED52), Skylab Program. NASA Life Sciences Data Archive. https://lsda.jsc.nasa.gov/Experiment/exper/428. Accessed 20 February 2018.

Miller, Michael. "Little charmers: UC biologists say wolf spiders have a wider range of personality than once believed." *UC Magazine*, University of Cincinnati. March 2017. <https://magazine.uc.edu/editors_picks/recent_features/wolfspider.html>

Milne, Lorus and Margery, and Susan Rayfield. *National Audubon Society Field Guide to North American Insects and Spiders.* Alfred A. Knopf, 1980.

Modlmeier, Andreas P., Kate L. Laskowski, Alex E. DeMarco, Anna Coleman, Katherine Zhao, Hayley A. Brittingham, Donna R. McDermott, and Jonathan N. Pruitt. "Persistent social interactions beget more pronounced personalities in a desert-dwelling social spider." *Biology Letters* Vol. 10, 2014.

Morley, Erica L., and Daniel Robert. "Electric fields elicit ballooning in spiders." *Current Biology* Vol. 28, 2018.

Morse, D.H. "Foraging patterns and time budgets of the crab spiders *Xysticus emertoni* Keyserling and *Misumena vatia* (Clerck) (Araneae: Thomisidae) on flowers." *Journal of Arachnology* Vol. 11, 1983.

Morse, Douglas H. "Excretion behavior of adult female crab spiders *Misumena vatia* (Araneae, Thomisidae)." *Journal of Arachnology* Vol. 36, 2008.

Nentwig, Wolfgang. "Parasitic fungi as a mortality factor of spiders." *Journal of Arachnology* Vol. 13, 1985.

Nitzsche, Rainar O.M. "Courtship, mating and agonistic behaviour in *Pisaura mirabilis* (Clerck, 1757)." *Bulletin of the British Arachnological Society* Vol. 15, 2011.

Novick, Laura R., Kefyn M. Catley, and Emily G. Schreiber. *Understanding Evolutionary History: An Introduction to Tree Thinking.* Version 3, 2010.

Nyffeler, Martin. "Ecological impact of spider predation: a critical assessment of Bristowe's and Turnbull's estimates." *Bulletin of the British Arachnological Society* Vol. 11, 2000.

Nyffeler, Martin, and Klaus Birkhofer. "An estimated 400–800 million tons of prey are annually killed by the global spider community." *The Science of Nature* Vol. 104, 2017.

Nyffeler, M., C.D. Dondale, and J.H. Redner. "Evidence for displacement of a North American spider, *Steatoda borealis* (Hentz), by the European species *S. bipunctata* (Linnaeus) (Araneae, Theridiidae)." *Canadian Journal of Zoology* Vol. 64, 1986.

Patil, Bhavani, Suphala Prabhu, and K.P. Rajashekharj. "Lyriform slit sense organs on the pedipalps and spinnerets of spiders." *Journal of Bioscience* Vol. 31, 2006.

Pekar, Stano, and Charles Haddad. "Trophic strategy of ant-eating *Mexcala elegans* (Araneae: Salticidae): looking for evidence of evolution of prey-specialization." *Journal of Arachnology* Vol. 39, 2011.

Poinar, G.O., Jr. "*Mermithid* (Nematoda) parasites of spiders and harvestmen." *Journal of Arachnology* Vol. 13, 1985.

Prokop Pavol, and Michael R. Maxwell. "Gift carrying in the spider *Pisaura mirabilis*: nuptial gift contents in nature and effects on male running speed and fighting success." *Animal Behaviour* Vol. 83, 2012.

Rand, the Rev. Silas Tertius. *Dictionary of the Language of the Micmac Indians, Who Reside in Nova Scotia, New Brunswick, Prince Edward Island, Cape Breton and Newfoundland.* Nova Scotia Printing Co., 1888.

Reillo, Paul R. "Mite parasitism of the polymorphic spider, *Enoplognatha ovata* (Araneae, Theridiidae) from coastal Maine." *Journal of Arachnology* Vol. 17, 1989.

Reillo, P.R., and D.H. Wise. "Black-stripe phenotypes in the spider *Enoplognatha ovata* (Araneae: Theridiidae)." *Journal of Arachnology* Vol. 15, 1987.

Roland, C., and J.S. Rovner. "Chemical and vibratory communication in the aquatic pisaurid spider *Dolomedes triton* (Araneae: Pisuaridae)." *Journal of Arachnology* Vol. 11, 1983.

Rovner, Jerome S. "Mechanisms controlling copulatory behavior in wolf spiders

(Araneae: Lycosidae)." *Psyche* Vol. 78, 1971.

—. "Morphological and ethological adaptations for prey capture in wolf spiders (Araneae, Lycosidae)." *Journal of Arachnology* Vol. 8, 1980.

—. Personal communications, 2014-2017.

Schwartz, Steven K., William E. Wagner, and Eileen Hebets. "Spontaneous male death and monogyny in the dark fishing spider." *Eileen Hebets Publications* Vol. 51, 2013.

Sentenska, Lenka, and Stano Pekar. "Eat or not to eat: reversed sexual cannibalism as a male foraging strategy in the spider *Micaria sociabilis* (Araneae: Gnaphosidae)." *Ethology* Vol. 120, 2014.

Settepani, Virginia, Trine Bilde, and Lena Grinsted. "Temporarily social spiders do not show personality-based task differentiation." *Animal Behavior* Vol. 105, 2015.

Shamble, Paul S., Gil Menda, James R. Golden, Eyal I. Nitzany, Katherine Walden, Tsevi Beatus, Damian O. Elias, Itai Cohen, Ronald N. Miles, and Ronald R. Hoy. "Airborne acoustic perception by a jumping spider." *Current Biology* Vol. 26, 2016.

Sierwald, Petra, and Jonathan A. Coddington. "Functional aspects of the male palpal organ in *Dolomedes tenebrosus*, with notes on the mating behavior (Araneae: Pisauridae)." *Journal of Arachnology* Vol. 16, 1988.

Sivalinghem, Senthurran, Michael M. Kasumovic, Andrew C. Mason, Maydianne C.B. Andrade, and Damian O. Elias. "Vibratory communication in the jumping spider *Phidippus clarus*: polyandry, male courtship signals, and mating success." *Behavioral Ecology*, 2010.

Skerl, Kevin L. "Spider conservation in the United States." www.umich.edu/~e-supdate/library/97.03-04/skerl.html

Stalhandske, Pia. "Nuptial gift in the spider *Pisaura mirabilis* maintained by sexual selection." *Behavioral Ecology* Vol. 12, 2001.

Stevenson, B.G., and D.L. Dindal. "Effect of leaf shape on forest litter spiders: community organization and microhabitat selection of immature *Enoplognatha ovata* (Clerck) (Theridiidae)." *Journal of Arachnology* Vol. 10, 1982.

Stoltz, J.A., D.O. Elias, and M.C.B. Andrade. "Females reward courtship by competing males in a cannibalistic spider." *Behavioral Ecology and Sociobiology* Vol. 62, 2008.

Stratton, Gail E., Eileen A. Hebets, Patricia R. Miller, and Gary L. Miller. "Pattern and duration of copulation in wolf spiders (Araneae: Lycosidae)." *Journal of Arachnology* Vol. 24, 1996.

Suttle, Kenwyn Blake. "The Evolution of Sexual Cannibalism." http://ib.berkeley.edu/courses/ib160/past_papers/suttle.html.

Tan, A.-M., R.G. Gillespie, and G.S. Oxford. "Paraphyly of the *Enoplognatha ovata* group (Araneae: Theridiidae) based on DNA sequences." *Journal of Arachnology* Vol. 27, 1999.

Tanaka, Kazuhiro. "Seasonal change in cold tolerance of the house spider, *Achaearanea tepidariorum* (Araneae: Theridiidae)." *Acta arachnologica* Vol. 42, 1993.

—. "Seasonal life cycle of the house spider, *Achaearana tepidariorum* (Araneae: Theridiidae) in northern Japan." *Applied Entomology and Zoology* Vol. 24, 1989.

Thoreau, H.D. The Writings of Henry D. Thoreau, Online Journal Transcripts, Manuscript Vol. 19 http://thoreau.library.ucsb.edu/writings_journals.html

Thorell, T. *Remarks on Synonyms of European Spiders* No. 1. Berling, 1870.

Tiedemann, Klaus B., Dora Fix Ventura, and Cesar Ades. "Spectral sensitivities of the eyes of the orb web spider *Argiope argentata* (Fabricius)." *Journal of Arachnology* Vol. 14, 1986.

Ubick, D., P. Paquin, P.E. Cushing, and V. Roth, eds., *Spiders of North America: An Identification Manual,* American Arachnological Society, 2017.

U.S. Fish & Wildlife Service. *Endangered Species.* www.fws.gov/endangered/

Vander Haegen, W. Matthew, and Daniel T. Jennings. "Spiders (Araneae) in the diet of American woodcock in Maine." *Journal of Arachnology* Vol. 18, 1990.

Vetter, Richard S. "Spiders of the genus *Loxosceles* (Araneae, Sicariidae): a review of biological, medical and psychological aspects regarding envenomations." *Journal of Arachnology* Vol. 36, 2008.

Vetter, Richard S., and Sean P. Bush. "The diagnosis of brown recluse spider bite is overused for dermonecrotic wounds of uncertain etiology." *Annals of Emergency Medicine* Vol. 39, 2002.

Vetter, Richard S., and Stoy A. Hedges. "Integrated pest management of the brown recluse spider." *Journal of Integrated Pest Management* Vol. 9, 2018.

Viera, C., and M.J. Albo. "Males of a subsocial spider choose among females of different ages and the same reproductive status." *Ethology Ecology & Evolution* Vol. 20, 2008.

Weber, Larry. *Spiders of the North Woods,* 2nd edition. Kolath and Stensass, 2013.

Weissmann, Monika, and Fritz Vollrath. "The effect of leg loss on orb-spider growth." *Bulletin of the British Arachnological Society* Vol. 11. 1998.

Wegner, Gerald S. *Spider Identification Guide.* BASF Corp., 2014.

Welbourn, W.C., and O.P. Young. "Mites parasitic on spiders, with a description of a new species of *Eutrombidium* (Acari, Eutrombidiidae)." *Journal of Arachnology* Vol. 16, 1988.

Whitehouse, Mary, Ingi Agnarsson, Tadashi Miyashita, Deborah Smith, Karen Cangialosi, Toshiya Masumoto, Daiqin Li, and Yann Henaut. "Argyrodes: phylogeny, sociality and interspecific interactions—a report on the *Argyrodes* Symposium, Badplaas 2001." *Journal of Arachnology* Vol. 30, 2002.

Wilde, Dana. "Humans in monsters' bodies." *The Maine Entomologist* (rpt.), Vol. 22, November 2018.

—. "*Pisaurina mira* in Maine." *The Maine Entomologist*, Vol. 21, May 2017.

—. "Spiders at Eagle Hill." *The Maine Entomologist*, Vol. 21, August 2017.

—. "Spiders in Maine." *Maine Boats, Homes & Harbors*, No. 124, 2013.

Wise, D.H. *Spiders in Ecological Webs*. Cambridge University Press. 1993.

Wise, David H., and Paul R. Reillo. "Frequencies of color morphs in four populations of *Enoplognatha ovata* (Araneae: Theridiidae) in eastern North America." *Psyche* Vol. 92, 1984.

Witt, P.N., et al. "Spider web-building in outer space : evaluation of records from the Skylab spider experiment." *Journal of Arachnology* Vol. 4, 1977.

Witt, Peter N. "Drugs alter web-building of spiders: a review and evaluation." *Behavioral Science* Vol. 16, January 1971.

Witt, Peter N., and Jerome S. Rovner, eds. *Spider Communication: Mechanisms and Ecological Significance*. Princeton University Press, 1982.

Wu, Chung-Huey, and Damian O. Elias. "Vibratory noise in anthropogenic habitats and its effect on prey detection in a web-building spider." *Animal Behaviour* Vol. 90, 2014.

Zschokke, Samuel. "Nomenclature of the orb-web." *Journal of Arachnology* Vol. 27, 1999.

—. "Ultraviolet reflectance of spiders and their webs." *Journal of Arachnology* Vol. 30, 2002.

Zurek, Daniel. "Spider Vision." <www.danielzurek.com/spider-vision.html>

Websites

BugGuide. https://bugguide.net

Encyclopedia of Life. http://eol.org

The Find-a-spider Guide for the Spiders of Southern Queensland. http://www.findaspider.org.au

International Union for Conservation of Nature Red List of Threatened Species. www.iucnredlist.org

Native American Spider Mythology. http://www.native-languages.org/legends-spider.htm

SpiderID. https://spiderid.com

Spiderz Rule http://www.spiderzrule.com

World Spider Catalog. www.wsc.nmbe.ch

Index of Spiders and Harvestmen

About the Author

Dana Wilde lives in Troy, Maine, and writes the Backyard Naturalist column which appears regularly in the *Kennebec Journal* and *Morning Sentinel* and occasionally in the *Sun Journal* newspapers, and originated in years past as the award-winning Amateur Naturalist column in the *Bangor Daily News*. He has been a college professor, editor, Fulbright scholar, and NEH fellow. He holds a bachelor's degree from the University of Southern Maine and doctoral and master's degrees from Binghamton University, where his doctoral dissertation was recognized as the Distinguished Dissertation in the Humanities and Fine Arts for 1995, in part for its efforts to bridge the "two cultures" of science and the humanities. His writings have appeared in *The Maine Entomologist* and many popular, literary, and scholarly publications; his books include *Summer to Fall: Notes and Numina from the Maine Woods* and *Nebulae: A Backyard Cosmography*. He is a member of the Maine Entomological Society, the International Society of Arachnology, and the National Book Critics Circle.

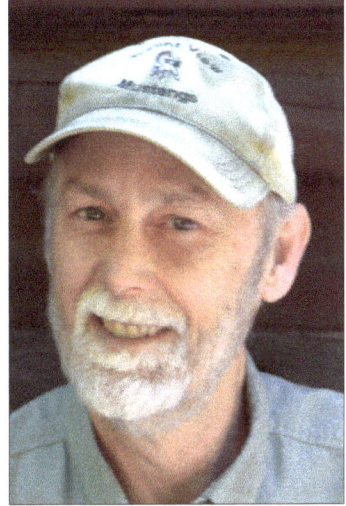

www.ingramcontent.com/pod-product-compliance
Lightning Source LLC
Chambersburg PA
CBHW040141270326
41928CB00022B/3281